Death and Hell

Death and Hell

AS REVEALED IN THE HOLY BIBLE

MAAFA DALIT

*And whosoever was not found written in the Book of Life was
cast into the Lake of Fire. Revelation 20:15*

Dedicated to
My Lord Jesus Christ- The Author of Life,
Who destroyed the power of death and hell
through His own bodily death
on the Cross for me. –Maafa Dalit-

Death and Hell

by Maafa Dalit
Copyright © by Mohan Mathews, pen name Maafa Dalit, 2010

ISBN: 978-0-9564732-0-2

Published by
Pilgrim Ministry
43 Wrenbury Avenue,
Withington, Manchester,
M20 1DR, England.
United Kingdom.
zionpilgrim@gmail.com
www.freewebs.com/maafadalit]

Printed and bound in India by
Authentic Media, Secunderabad 500 055
E-mail: printing@ombooks.org

My God, I Love Thee
17th cent. ; translated by Edward Caswall

My God, I love thee, not because
I hope for heaven thereby,
nor yet because, if I love not,
I must forever die.

Thou, O my Jesus, thou didst me
upon the cross embrace;
for me didst bear the nails and spear
and manifold disgrace.

Then why, O blessed Jesus Christ,
should I not love thee well?
Not for the sake of winning heaven,
nor of escaping hell.

Not with the hope of gaining aught,
not seeking a reward,
but as thyself hast loved me,
everlasting Lord.

So would I love thee, dearest Lord,
and thy praise will sing;
because thou art my loving God
and my eternal King.

Death And Hell

As revealed in the Holy Bible

But the fearful, and unbelieving and the abominable, and murderers, and whoremongers, and sorcerers and idolaters, and all liars, shall have their part in the lake that burns with fire and brimstone: which is the Second Death.
Revelation 21. 8

Considering the truth that The Bible is the Only Book in the world that clearly tells us Who God IS, Who the Devil is, Who we are, What Heaven and Hell are like and the Eternal Destiny of the Saved and the Lost, it is a profound tragedy that the Bible is being sold, instead of being distributed freely. Though the Bible is the most printed and most translated book, it is not the most read book. There is also too much heartless and religious reading of Scripture. The Bible has been copyrighted and wronged by proliferating versions.

Dedication

This book is an offering to the Lord who purchased my soul from the slave market of sin, from Satan, Death and Hell. The book is the fruit of my sincere repentance of the darkest sin of my life viz., the sin of abortion. May God- the God and Father of the Lord Jesus Christ help us never to forget that Hell is a reality and transform all the hells in our hearts into the Heaven that is the Presence of Jesus. This book will be sold at a price that will only cover the production and shipping cost. Let us dedicate the rest of our life to the knowledge of our Saviour and God and let the Heaven that is Jesus in our hearts spread abroad the sweet fragrance of Eternal Life.

How to read this book
Please read this book with a copy of the Holy Bible alongside, to check the veracity of the truths that are documented in these pages. Kindly read slowly and prayerfully. Say a small prayer quietly, in your own words for me and all readers of this book that we may learn to live and die with dignity and compassion, fulfilling the unique purpose of God for every human being, uniquely created in the image of God.

After reading
Kindly do not let this copy of the book have any rest. Circulate the book.

Contents

Preface

A good name is better than precious ointment;
and the day of death than the day of one's birth.
Ecclesiastes 7:1

The value, functions and properties of the soul are such that the entrance of even a single soul into hellfire is a tragedy of awesome proportions. This book is not prepared due to any form of morbid fascination with death. It is the result of a God given desire to study and understand what the Bible says about the common destiny of spiritual death, biological death and second death.

God has confirmed the truth of Holy Scripture that an everlasting burning hellfire is a real destination for those who reject the life in Jesus Christ. Hell is the terminus, the last stop for the vast numbers of my fellow human beings on the broad road to everlasting destruction. This heart-rending truth is the motivating factor that has produced this book. It is the same motivation that led many missionaries and martyrs to lay down their lives for the sake of Christ and His gospel.

Death- An Unnecessary Taboo

In 1998, when my Papa was at the threshold of death, I failed to plainly reassure and comfort him that Our Lord Jesus would come and take him home. I refused to face up to the fact that death of the body was imminent. As far as I know, no one else in the family, talked to him about dying either. This is the taboo and tragedy of this world that most families (Christian and otherwise) never talk about death and dying as naturally as they would talk about life- both of this life and the life to come. The irony of this is even greater, in view of the fact that we are surrounded by forces of biological and spiritual death, within and without.

Since then, my Heavenly Father, the Father and God of the Lord Jesus Christ has imparted abundant showers of His love and mercy. He has graciously revealed the reality of the second death, or the eternal separation of the ungodly from the Presence of God.

Scaring you or Warning you?

There are some people that may say it is wrong to scare a person into heaven. They are wrong. It is written, "And of some have compassion, making a difference; and others save with fear, pulling them out of the FIRE; hating even the garment spotted by the flesh". Jude 22,23.

This message may be considered as a road sign of

warning. Some may look at a sign that reads, "The bridge is out," and say, "Oh, someone is just trying to scare us into taking another road. Let's go on the same way." They go on and plunge to their death. The sign was not meant to scare people. It was meant to warn people of impending danger. Likewise, this message is intended to warn people of impending danger, unless they repent.

The rich man will be there. Many preachers, Sunday school teachers, church choir singers, and even missionaries will be there. Consider carefully. Most people that have ever lived will be there. Only a few shall receive eternal life and forever be with the Lord.

The Tragic Deception at Funerals
The richer the deceased, the more elaborate and expensive are the coffin, the funerary rites, and religious ceremonies. So often when a person dies, people will say, "He has gone to a better place now." They don't understand that most people perish to hell, not to heaven. While they are thinking that person has gone to a better place, the departed souls are actually crying out in torment words like, "I AM TORMENTED IN THIS FLAME." Indeed, Satan does deceive the whole world.

The Sin of Abortion
God has forgiven my sin of abortion of a baby girl. The

medical authorities of Copenhagen deemed it good to kill our baby due to Down's syndrome. We made a deadly decision, in consenting to their advice to kill the foetus due to Down's syndrome. The sin of murdering an innocent soul certainly makes one worthy of hellfire. The open confession of sin by a penitent heart causes the record in heaven to be wiped clean by the blood of Jesus. The eternal destination of Hell and the heinous sin of abortion are now two things I wish to warn every person under the sun to flee from.

Brevity of Life

The brevity of earthly life cannot be over emphasized. The Bible refers to the earthly life as a vapour, a shadow, grass and the flower of the grass, etc., Modern living gives the deceitful impression to the wealthy and educated that we are here to stay and that this life is almost endless. Moses the great man of God (about whom God said that He spoke with face to face as a man speaks to his friend), says in Psalm 90: 9, 10, 12 that we spend our years as a tale that is told. He asks God to teach us to number our days (not years!) so that we may apply our hearts to wisdom. God has kept the time of our death outside our knowledge. But the godly and the faithful can enter death in blissful sleep in full anticipation of the Heavenly Reward.

Sleeping Christians
The Church is virtually asleep and right through history there has been a Christian religion like any other religion that does not cost any sacrifice with the ritual of Sunday worship, as though other days are less holy for God. The need to evangelise the world is largely ignored and the call of God for ministry is considered by many Christians to be only for church leaders and missionaries. Many study at bible colleges for the sake of using titles like Pastor and Reverend, to get the honour of men, not to hide behind the Cross of Christ in a self-effacing lifestyle. There is more Churchianity and not enough Christianity, which is why the world is still not evangelised, more than 2000 years after Christ.

Christians Beware !
While Christendom seems to have rocked itself to sleep on the truths about hell and damnation, let the man or woman who fears God, tremble as the words of Jesus ring in our ears: "He that overcomes shall not be hurt by the second death", clearly implying that the one who does not overcome may be hurt by the second death, or lose the salvation that he was expected to consolidate and endure unto the end for the final salvation of soul and body. This book is meant to sound the trumpet for Christians and unbelievers alike that hell is as much a reality as heaven,

both in this world, in the unbelieving heart, as well as being an eternal destination.

God- Source of all Goodness

God is the Father of Life and free spirits. The testimony of our very being, the faculties of our spirit, soul and body clearly reveal the loving hand of the Good Father in Heaven. Life and every desirable thing come from the God who created every molecule that we see, feel, enjoy and misuse. The riches of this world and the pleasures of sin are deeply deceitful that attempt to deny God and His laws.

God has put His seal on every atom and living cell in creation that He is an Almighty and All-wise Person worthy of worship. And yet man refuses to do that which is obviously required of him, viz., to seek and worship God.

God is so good that He sends sunshine and rain even on those who hate Him. True life- biological, spiritual and eternal life, all spring from the fountain of the Prince of Life. There will be plenty of opportunity in Hell, for those who hate God to reflect over the goodness of God and the folly of their soul in rejecting Him.

Hell and Heaven- Equally Eternal Realities

Those who do not consciously possess Christ are citizens

in the land of the dead here on earth already and hell is the condition of their heart whether they have Christian names or not, or worship at a cathedral or chapel on every Sunday of the year.

Hell is God reluctantly granting non-Christians their wish. Non-Christians push Jesus aside, yet in his extravagant love Jesus keeps giving and giving. They do not want him meddling in their lives, but he keeps forcing himself upon them, showering them with gifts of life and pleasure.

In hell they finally get their way. To be granted separation from the Source of every good and beautiful thing, however, is a terrifying prospect. The only way of truly knowing that God is love is through the revelation of Jesus and the Bible, both of which lovingly and emphatically warn of hell's grim reality.

FORGIVENESS = HEAVEN

Forgiveness is Heaven. Unforgiveness is Hell. God exposed a king in the Old Testament of the Bible, called David, through the prophet Nathan. The dual sin of David in the premeditated murder of his own loyal soldier and adultery with his wife has been published in the Word of God settled in heaven and in over 400 languages around the world. Jesus Christ- the Son of David (!), is the Lord from Heaven, before whose piercing eyes we are bone-naked.

Forgiveness of sins does not come with any magic incantation in Hebrew or Sanskrit. It does not come with a dip in the Jordan or Ganges.

Circumcised in Heart = True Jews

A Roman spear pierced open the very Heart of God powered by the sins of all humanity. Thus the way into Heaven has been opened for anyone and everyone to become a true Jew. A true Jew is a soul that sees Christ crucified for his or her sins on the Cross of Calvary. This causes the heart of the believer to be circumcised. An Israelite is one who speaks Hebrew, or worships at a synagogue, a foreigner who converts to Judaism or one who is born as the child of a father or mother who is of the fleshly seed of Abraham. But a true Jew, is of the spiritual seed of Abraham in whom all the families of the earth have been blessed. A true Jew worships Jesus Christ of Nazareth- the Crucified King. This circumcision causes a child of Adam to become a child of God and to be born into the land of the living.

Blood of Christ on Conscience = Forgiveness

Secular books of history do not accord any significance to the death of Jesus of Nazareth. The eternal truth however, is that God died in the flesh and His Blood not only flowed out in time and the fleshly body of the Son of God, it continues to flow in the spirit realm onto the conscience of the believer and the record of sins in Heaven. This is a holy and real phenomenon that takes place in the spirit realm.

This is the fulfilment of every animal sacrifice man has ever made, including the Old Testament shadow of the sacrifice of bulls and goats. The Holy Spirit re-enacts the Death of Jesus that took place in history to the eyes of the believer, so that I can see it happening before me right here and now.

Millions of sons and daughters of Adam have experienced the joyful liberation that comes with the assurance of God's forgiveness. God pardons sin by sprinkling His Divine Blood on the conscience when we come in humble faith, in repentance and open confession of sins. Sin that is 'hidden' in the heart or life, not confessed to God will torment the soul.

The Blood of Jesus is the ransom that was paid to redeem souls from both the second death in hell and for some- even the corruption of the body in the grave. See Hosea 13:14 I will ransom them from the power of the grave; I will redeem them from death: O death, I will be thy plagues; O grave, I will be thy destruction:

True Worshipper = Jew
As Jesus told the Samaritan woman at the well: Salvation is

of the Jews and we must know Whom or What we worship. The Bible says that idolaters and all liars (including the covetous or greedy) will end up in Hell. Anyone who does not worship the Father in Heaven, the God of Our Lord Jesus Christ, the Invisible God in spirit and truth from the heart in acknowledgement of one's sins and the atonement of Jesus, is not worshipping the One True God.

Dear reader, deeply loved of God, come as you are to the Father of all free spirits, through Jesus Christ and know that He is waiting to flood your heart with His Divine, Unconditional Love. God has blessed every family of the earth through Abraham, through the True Spiritual seed of Jesus Christ. You are welcome to the Commonwealth of the Israel (Family) of God.

Faith in the Creation Account

Many Christians are not completely convinced in the veracity of the Bible account of Creation and the Fall of Adam and thus of all mankind. I was one of them until 1988. If you believe that Jesus is your Saviour, it requires that you believe in Him as the Last Adam who paid the price of death to bring eternal life to any of the children of the First Adam. The same Bible tells us, that there is an eternal place of flames and torment where some will suffer everlasting separation from the Goodness; we call God, in the English vernacular.

Darkness Abounds
Secular education, modern technologies and the media, the teaching of evolution, have all bloated the pride of life so that the arrogance will be addressed by divine retribution. Knowledge and information of the material world is increasing at a tremendous pace. But atheism and ungodliness are also abounding on every side.

Satan and billions of his demons are busy alienating God's choice creation- the children of Adam, the offspring of God. The darkness gets thicker and fills the world on every side. Though it is written that light will break forth suddenly, Jesus also asks us whether He will find faith, as the love of many grows cold in the last days, just before His Appearing.

Braving Death and Hell
The Authorized or King James Version of the Bible refers to Sheol, Hades and Gehenna, all as Hell. The word "Hell" is derived from the Saxon 'helan', to cover; hence the covered or the invisible place. The terms are explained in this book. The bravest people are not those who make great discoveries and inventions or climb Mount Everest. The bold and the brave are the Christians who challenge Satan, Hell and Death and live each day as though it was their last day in the world.

No Sacred Language, Country or Culture

There is no language that is sacred in itself, whether Hebrew, Tamil, Sanskrit or Greek. It is the expression of the heart that is holy or unholy. When the beloved man of God, John Wycliffe first translated the Bible into common English, he began a glorious revolution of bringing access to the sacred Word of God down to the common person. The band of good men called Lollards who worked with him, spread the light of literacy as well, in dark and illiterate Britain of the 12th century.

Since then, thousands of bible translators have laboured in dark and distant lands to bring the light and life of the Gospel. William Carey cancelled a church service so that he could quickly translate the order that would ban widow burning (or sati) in Bengal. Carey loved India and his mortal coil is buried in Kolkata. Hudson Taylor declared: If I had a thousand lives, I would give them all for China. The love of Christ transcends the conceited pride of national identity and cultural heritage of one's birth and upbringing.

When Jesus says that He is Alpha and Omega, you will be a fool to think that He is glorifying Hellenistic culture or that the Way of Jesus is a European religion. Salvation is of the Jews, but not only for Jews for God is a Spirit. God is not a man that He should lie.

Hell will Declare that God is Good

The consummation of all Creation and Re-Creation is in Christ, through His Word, His Sufferings, His Death, His Resurrection and Glorification. By Him every form of Existence finds purpose and form in Heaven and on Earth. God is Good to ALL and His Mercy endures forever. Even Death and Hell will glorify God! So be it (Amen).

Chapter One
Death-The Great
Common Denominator

Death: Science cannot stop it.
Riches cannot avoid it.

There was a man whose doctor informed him he had only a short time to live. He dreaded the thought of just an "ordinary death" and dreamed of dying for some heroic cause. Then, his chance came!

A robbery took place in his town. The police had the store surrounded, but the robber was holding hostages inside. The man told the police chief that he would like to go in and rescue the hostages. The chief said, "You will be killed!" The man replied, "I am not afraid. You see, I am going to die soon anyway."

With permission, the man walked boldly into the store and headed straight toward the thief. The robber was so shocked by the man's boldness that he assumed others were also in the store and surrendered—releasing his hostages!

A few days later, the doctor called the man back and told him, "I misread your test results. You will not be dying soon." The man then lost his boldness as he focused once again on living rather than dying.

Death Began when Eternal Life Ended

Most people live in ignorance of the truth that death has not always existed, neither the death of the spirit nor the death of the body. Many others consider that bodily death is the permanent extinction of all life and consciousness. This is a terrible and tragic illusion, as not one person born into this world will ever disappear forever in terms of human consciousness. All creation is longing to be delivered from the vanity of death, decay and corruption. Were it not for sin, death had never had a beginning, and were it not for death, sin would never have had an ending.

Death- End of all Living

Death is the Ultimate humiliation of Wickedness, Strength, Wealth, Health, Wisdom and Beauty. The humbling effect of death is called the dust of death in Psalm 22:15.

Psalm 89:48 says: "What man is he that liveth, and shall not see death? Shall he deliver his soul from the hand of the grave" In Isaiah 38:18 the prophet says: "...the grave cannot praise thee, death can not celebrate thee: they that go down into the pit cannot hope for thy truth."

Enoch- Not dead yet!
Faith in God was instrumental even in the Dispensation of Conscience, whereby Enoch pleased God and was translated without seeing death as an exceptionally rare individual who walked with God in perfect harmony (See Hebrews 11:5). The body of Enoch is being preserved in supernatural manner for more than 4000 years. It is believed that Enoch will return to the earth one day to die in his body. May God grant us also the grace to walk with Him and please Him by our faith.

Mortal Life is Ephemeral
It is true that the Bible compares human life to a shadow, a passing vapour, a wind that cometh not again.., and so forth. But all these are terms referring to the brevity of biological life of the mortal body of flesh on earth. This does not in any may undermine the eternal value of the human soul. The wealth of the whole world is considered by Jesus to be of less value than the price of one's soul.

Wealth of No Avail
In the following verses we read how the wealth of this world is of no use in the hour of death and without any power to save from damnation:

They that trust in their wealth, and boast themselves in the multitude of their riches; None of them can by any means redeem his brother, nor give to God a ransom for him: (For the redemption of their soul is precious, and it ceases for ever:) Psalm 49:6-12.

Treasures of wickedness profit nothing: but righteousness delivers from death. Proverbs 10:2

Riches profit not in the day of wrath: but righteousness delivers from death. Proverbs 11:4

Worldly Wise and Honourable

Psalm 49:12, 20 say that even if man has an honourable status in this world, if he lacks spiritual understanding, is like the beasts that perish. God calls the foolish, weak, base, despised and nought to bring to nothing the mighty and the worldly wise (I Corinthians 1: 26-29). No flesh will boast in the presence of God.

Skin Beauty is Vain

The skin-deep beauty of the vain people of the world will be brought to nothing at the grave. Psalm 49:14 says that they are laid low in the grave and death will feed on them and that their beauty will be consumed in the grave. Through the centuries, the sun, the rain, the wind, worms, decay, fire and destruction have fed on the superficial beauty of women, the strength of men and the works of art and architecture of men, while saints of inner beauty have been welcomed to their imperishable home in heaven.

Travails of Death

In Job 30:23, righteous Job speaks of death as the house appointed for all living and Job 38:17 the gates of death and the doors of the shadow of death are mentioned. David pleads that God may lift him from the gates of death in Psalm 9.13 and in Psalm 23.4 he speaks of the comfort of God when he walks through the valley of the shadow of death.

In I Samuel 15:32, the bitterness of death is spoken of and in 2 Samuel 22:5 David speaks of the waves of death as compassing him. In 2 Samuel 22:6, the sorrows of hell (In Psalm 18:4 it is called the sorrows of death) and the snares of death are spoken of in the same vein. In Psalm 55.4 we read of the terrors of death. In Job 24:17, we read of the terrors of the shadow of death. God has prepared the instruments of death for the wicked we read in Psalm 7:13.

Death as a domain is called the land of darkness and the valley of the shadow of death in Job 10:21 and in Psalm 23:4.

The firstborn of death is referred to in Job 18:13 as devouring the physically strong. Job 28:3 speaks of something called the stones of darkness.

The prophet Jeremiah warns the Jews and us: Give glory to the LORD your God, before he cause darkness, and before your feet stumble upon the dark mountains, and, while ye look for light, he turn it into the shadow of death, and make it gross darkness. Jeremiah 13:16

Death knows the Wisdom of God
The poetic words of Job, the ancient sage writing about the great treasure of wisdom implies that even death and destruction owe their reality to the wisdom of God. Destruction and death say, We have heard the fame (of Wisdom) thereof with our ears. Job 28:22

Hating Wisdom is to Love Death
In Proverbs 8:35, 36 We read Wisdom (Jesus Christ) saying that he who finds wisdom finds life and favour, and that he who sins against Wisdom wrongs against his own soul and that all who hate wisdom are actually loving death.

The Truly Wise prepare daily for death
If men are prepared to die they are ready for anything. There is nothing more certain than death, nothing more uncertain than the time of dying. I will therefore be prepared at all times for that which may come at any time. It ought to be the business of every person, every day, to prepare for our last day. Death and what is beyond it will show who was wise and who was a fool. While bodily death is an assured certainty, very few prepare for this occasion.

Death can strike at any moment and the worldly lifestyle gives almost everyone the illusion that death is for others and for one who has reached a ripe old age or for the occasional victim of a terminal illness or accident.

Never for me, thinks the fool. That person is wise who has made every preparation for death and is living each day as though it were his last.

Greater the sinner, greater the saint
God does not take pleasure in the death even of the wicked. When we die, we leave behind us all that we have and take with us all that we are. It has sometimes been laid down as a sort of maxim,"The greater the sinner, the greater the saint;" as if to have a full measure of Christ's cup, a man must first have drunken deeply of the cup of devils. Though such a doctrine is simply wicked and detestable; however, this is known among God's children that no degree of sin, however extreme precludes the acquisition of any degree of holiness, however high. No sinner so great, but he may, through God's grace, become a saint ever so great.

A true Christian is in the workshop of God where the revolutionary transformation is underway quenching the fires of hell in the heart. God expects sincerity in our approach to the Salvation in Jesus. All other virtues He will freely impart through the knowledge of the matchless love of God in Jesus Christ Our Lord. He is purifying my heart and mind of every rivulet and stream of hell, establishing heaven in my spirit and soul.

Hell and Heaven- Eternal Condition/Destination

At clinical or bodily death, the spirit will return to God who granted life and the soul will go to its destination in Heaven (a Place with the Perfect Presence of God) or Hell (Place of Wrath of Omnipotent Majesty). The Psalmist says: Your heart (the seat of desire) shall live forever (Psalm 22:26). In other words, the condition of the heart at death will continue into all eternity. In Jesus- the Only Sinless Man, the Son of God in the flesh, tasted the hellish separation from the Father and the death of His fleshly body, for every person born into this world. Thus rejecting Jesus is tantamount to choosing Hell.

The death of the body is no reason for a Christian to grieve. On the contrary, the Early Christians actually rejoiced and celebrated the death of believers. Their whole lifestyle turned the world upside down and proved that Jesus was Risen from the dead. Their faith was not just an empty intellectual confession or yet another dead religion.

Psychopannychia or Soul Sleep: There are those like the Jehovah's Witnesses, Seventh Day Adventists etc., who have been influenced by a cultic view called psychopannychia, more famously known as soul sleep. The idea is that at death the soul goes into a state of suspended animation. It remains in slumber, in an unconscious state, until it is awakened at the time of the great resurrection. The soul is still alive, but it is unconscious, so that there is no consciousness of the passing of time. This conclusion is drawn improperly from the way in which the New Testament speaks about people in death being asleep. The common Jewish expression that they are "asleep" means they are enjoying the reposed, peaceful tranquillity of those who have passed beyond the struggles of this world and into the presence of God.

See elsewhere in this book for a more in-depth discussion of this topic.

We may aptly conclude this chapter with the word of the Lord to all the living that they can turn from death to life, from Ezekiel 18:32 "For I have no pleasure in the death of him that dieth, saith the Lord GOD: wherefore turn yourselves, and live ye."

Chapter Two
Biological Life And Death

Biblical Aspects Of Life and Death

Most people do not study the Bible in depth today. This is a monumental tragedy, since only the Bible tells us how we all got here, and where we are going! As with most concepts, the simplest and best way to understand anything is to go back to the beginning. According to the Bible, our physical bodies are composed of the same elements as the dust of the Earth.

The LORD God (Jesus Christ) formed the first living human being, called Adam (Man), as recorded in Genesis 2:7: "And the LORD God formed man of the dust of the ground, and breathed into his nostrils the breath of life; and man became a living being."

Our human bodies were originally created out of dust. It is interesting to note that the chemical components of the human body are exactly the same chemical elements as the dust of the ground. Our physical bodies are made up of 17 chemical elements. In fact these are the same 17 elements that are found in the dust of the ground. It is a matter of common observation that, after a body has been cremated, only dust remains.

The Spirit enters at Conception

Our bodies also contain a human spirit, which is essential for life. According to the Bible, human beings are all human spirits living in physical bodies. We are told that the human spirit is infused into the body of a baby while it is in its mother's womb. This is described in Ecclesiastes 11:5, "God's ways are as mysterious as the pathway of the wind and as the manner in which a human spirit is infused into the little body of a baby while it is yet in its mother's womb," TLB.

According to James 2:26 a body without an indwelling spirit is dead. A baby's body cannot live without an indwelling spirit. The human spirit must therefore enter the body of the baby at conception.

The Bible does not deny the physical death of the human body, but states that there is more to the death of a human being than the death of the physical body.

Jesus Christ is the Giver of Life

Approximately 2,000 years ago Jesus Christ became a

Human Being. But before that Jesus Christ was a Spirit, as confirmed in the following Scriptures:

Genesis 1:1: "In the beginning God created the Heavens and the Earth."

John 1:1-4: "In the beginning was the Word (Jesus Christ), and the Word was with God, and the Word was God. He was in the beginning with God. All things were made through Him, and without Him nothing was made that was made. In Him was life, and the life was the light of men."

Colossians 1:15-17, "Christ is the exact likeness of the unseen God. He existed before God made anything at all, and, in fact, Christ himself is the Creator who made everything in Heaven and Earth, the things we can see and the things we can't; the spirit world with its kings and kingdoms, its rulers and authorities; all were made by Christ for his own use and glory. He was before all else began and it is his power that holds everything together," TLB.

Physical, Biological or Clinical death

The Bible states in James 2:26, "The body without the spirit is dead". In other words, no human life can exist without the indwelling spirit. The spirit enters the human body at conception, and leaves the human body at death. This is clearly illustrated in the following sections.

The following passage is taken from Ecclesiastes 12:6-7, "Remember your Creator now while you are young-before the silver cord of life snaps and the gold bowl is broken; before the pitcher is broken at the fountain and the wheel is broken at the cistern; then the dust returns to the earth as it was, and the spirit returns to God who gave it" TLB. This passage confirms that at death the human spirit returns to God who gave it.

This says that at death the human body decomposes, but the spirit (which is indestructible) returns to God. This means that the "real you" is a soul that will live forever.

When the heart and the brain cease functioning, clinical death is decreed. Atheists believe that biological death leads to the extinction of all properties of the mind.

'Sleep' as a metaphor of bodily death
The death (of the body) is described by the metaphor of sleep. The Psalmist in Psalm 13:3 asks God to hear him and lighten his ..eyes, lest I sleep the sleep of death. In the Shepherd Psalm, the great comfort of the believer is expressed in the lack of fear, even while walking through the valley of the shadow of death. Psalm 23.4. Job and Daniel also spoke of the dead as 'sleeping in the dust' (Job 7.21; 14.12). Daniel records the future resurrection of those who ......sleep in the dust of the earth shall awake,

some to everlasting life, and some to shame and everlasting contempt (Daniel 12:2).

Reincarnation refuted
Souls of men are born once and after the death of the body, they await judgment at the resurrection of their everlasting body. This we see clearly in Heb 9:27 "And as it is appointed unto men once to die, but after this the judgment".

We are told in Hebrews 9:27, "It is appointed for men to die once, but after this the judgment". When the physical body dies, our spirit will live on, and will be sent either to Heaven or to Hell, according to our relationship with Jesus Christ. There were two thieves crucified with Jesus Christ. One is now in Heaven, and the other in Hell.

Jesus Christ said, in John 5:25-29, "I solemnly declare that the time is coming, in fact, it is here, when the dead shall hear my voice-the voice of the Son of God-and those who listen shall live. The Father has life in himself, and has granted his Son to have life in himself, and to judge the sins of all mankind because he is the Son of Man. Don't be so surprised! Indeed the time is coming when all the dead in their graves shall hear the voice of God's Son, and shall rise again-those who have done good, to eternal life; and those who have continued in evil, to judgment," TLB.

Confirming Clinical Death

When a patient dies a doctor will normally certify that the patient is dead. If the doctor knows the patient, and the cause of death is known, the doctor will normally issue a Death Certificate, usually with a second doctor.

If the cause of death is not known, or uncertain, the doctor will normally refer the case to the local Coroner's Officer. A pathologist, who will ascertain the cause of death on the basis of post mortem findings, will then usually conduct a post mortem examination. Doctors are invariably very familiar with the examination of dead bodies to certify death. These are the physical signs that a doctor will normally look for to certify death:

• Examination of the Cardiovascular System: No pulse may be felt at a major blood vessel, such as the carotid artery in the neck. On auscultation of the heart with a stethoscope no heart sounds are heard. If an ECG machine (Electrocardiogram) is connected to the heart, no electrical activity may be detected at the heart, and there is a characteristic flat line tracing on the monitor.

• Examination of the Respiratory System: There are no respiratory movements of the chest wall. On auscultation of the chest with a stethoscope no respiratory sounds may be heard. If the patient is connected to a ventilating machine, there are no voluntary movements of the patient's respiratory system detectable on the machine's breathing bag.

• Examination of the Nervous System: The pupils become dilated due to lack of tone of the muscles of the iris. There are no skeletal muscle reflexes. If an EEG machine (Electroencephalogram) is connected to the brain, no electrical activity may be detected from the brain, and the characteristic electrical brain waves are flat.

Chapter Three
Death Penalty
In The Old Testament

It is of much value to consider the nature of the offences for which the Jews suffered capital punishment or the death sentence in the Old Testament. While the New Testament does not permit the death sentence for any offence, it offers the possibility to any soul and every soul for receiving eternal life through repentance and confession of sin to God, and faith in Jesus Christ as Saviour and Lord. John the Apostle writes about a sin that is worthy of death, but does not describe exactly which sin it is that carries that consequence.

Not Seeking God:
Whosoever that would not seek the LORD God of Israel should be put to death, whether small or great, whether man or woman (2 Chronicles 15:13).

Mount Sinai and Mount Zion Contrasted
In Exodus 19:12 (And thou shalt set bounds unto the people round about, saying, Take heed to yourselves, that

ye go not up into the mount, or touch the border of it: whosoever toucheth the mount shall be surely put to death:)

Moses was instructed to tell the people of Israel that they were not to touch Mount Sinai when God would descend upon it. This speaks of the glorious holiness of God. Death and condemnation were ministered by the Law that was revealed by God through Moses in the Old Testament. In the New Testament, Paul says that we have come to Mount Zion in Heaven that may be touched and where grace and life are ministered. If the ministration of death was so glorious that Moses had to veil his face (2 Corinthians 3:7), the ministration of life is far more glorious.

Law of Honouring Parents: In Exodus 21:15 we read that if a person beat a man, or his or her father or mother, they were to be put to death. He who cursed his father or mother was also to be put to death (Exodus 21:17; Leviticus 20:9). Jesus confirmed the importance of honouring one's parents, also in the New Testament, in Matthew 15:24 and Mark 7:10.

Law of Men Stealing and Traffic in Human Beings: In Exodus 21:16, the stealing and trading in human beings carried the death penalty.

Law of Conjugal Relations: A man or woman who had sexual relations with a beast was to be put to death and the beast was to be killed (Exodus 22:19; Leviticus 20:15,16). The adulterer and adulteress were to be killed (Leviticus 20:10).

A man who lies with his stepmother or daughter-in-law was to be killed for the confusion that was created (Leviticus 20:10,11,12). If a man lies with another man in homosexual relations, they were to be killed (Leviticus 20:13).

Law of the Sabbath or the Seventh Day: The Israelites were commanded to keep the Sabbath and whosoever who does any work or defiles the Sabbath was to be killed (Exodus 31:14,15).

Law of Homicide decreed death to any man who fatally assaulted or killed anyone (Exodus 21:12; Leviticus 24:17,21). However, two or three witnesses were needed for conviction. One witness was not sufficient to convict a person of murder (See Numbers 35:30; Deuteronomy 17:6).

Moreover in Numbers 35:16, 17, 18, 31, we also read that a compensation was not to be had from one convicted of murder, but the murderer must on every occasion be put to death. In Deuteronomy 24:16 God decrees that the fathers should not be put to death for the children, neither shall the children be put to death for the fathers, but that every man should be put to death for his own sin.

Wizards and Mediums Stoned: Magicians and people with familiar spirits were to be stoned to death (Leviticus 20:27).

Child Sacrifice Forbidden: The Israelite or stranger who offered his child as a sacrifice to the idol of Molech was to be stoned to death by the people of the land (Leviticus 20:2). Clarke's commentary notes that this idol was probably an emblematic personification of the solar influence, as made of brass, in the form of a man, with the head of an ox; that a fire was kindled in the inside, and the child to be sacrificed to him was put in his arms, and roasted to death.

Blasphemy: One who blasphemes the Name of the Lord is to be stoned to death by the congregation of Israel as well as by the stranger in their midst (Leviticus 24:16).

Person dedicated to God cannot be Redeemed: Every man who is devoted shall surely be put to death; or, as some understand it, be the Lord's property, or be employed in his service, till death. (Leviticus 27:29).

Stranger approaching Tabernacle: In Numbers 1:51 and Numbers 3:38 we read that the foreigner who approaches the tabernacle when it is being pitched or taken down, is to be put to death. Moses and Aaron and his sons were to camp eastward and keep the charge of the sanctuary.

A Stranger approaching the High Priest (Aaron and his sons) as they wait on their priestly office should be put to death (Numbers 3:10; 18:7).

Rebellion against Joshua was to be stopped by the death sentence (Joshua 1:18).

Breach of Sabbath law in the instance of the man who was found gathering sticks on the Sabbath was punished stoning to death (Numbers 15:35)

Earth opens to swallow Korah, Dathan and Abiram
The challenge of the authority and election of Moses and Aaron by the company of Korah among the people of Israel, led to the instantaneous and sudden judgment of death by the earth opening up to swallow the rebels and their property.

False prophet or seer to be put to death: In Chapter 13 of Deuteronomy, there is an account of how to destroy the false prophets and those who may try to seduce Israel to serve foreign gods, whether individuals or peoples.

A Rapist was to be killed if the rape was done in the countryside, where the cry of the woman could not be heard (Deuteronomy 22: 25, 26).

Stubborn, Rebellious, Gluttonous or Drunken Sons were to be stoned to death (Deuteronomy 21:18-21).

Sundry laws: At the Feast of Unleavened Bread, the Israelites were not to have leaven in the house for seven days. Anyone who ate leaven was "cut off from Israel" (See Exodus 12:15.).

The owner of an ox who does not restrain an ox that had earlier been reported for goring people was to be punished with the death penalty and the ox was to be stoned to death (Exodus 21:29).

If a man was killed by capital punishment by hanging on a tree, the corpse was to be taken down before nightfall (Deuteronomy 21:22). The body was not to be left on the tree through the night.

Among the cities given to the Levites in the land of Canaan, six of them were to be set apart for those who commit unintentional manslaughter to flee to, where he was to stay until the death of the high priest. The revenger could kill the manslayer if he was found outside the borders of the city of refuge (Numbers 35:25, 27, 28; Deuteronomy 19:1-10).

Shedding of blood defiled the land and it was cleansed only by the blood of him that shed it, in the case of outright murder (Numbers 35:33).

Idolaters or worshippers of the sun, moon or anything of the host of heaven was to be stoned to death, first by the two or three witnesses and then by the hands of all the people. Idolatry was considered to be an abomination (Deuteronomy 17:2-7)

In the book of Ezra, we read in Chapter 7, about the

King Artaxerxes sending the decree that whosoever would not do the law of the God of Israel or the law of the king, judgment of death, banishment, confiscation of goods or imprisonment was to be carried out.

In the book of Esther chapter 5, we see the Queen Esther entering the inner court of the king contrary to the decree that said that anyone to whom the king did not extend the golden sceptre would be put to death. She boldly takes the ultimate risk for saving her people from death.

In the book of Daniel chapter three, the three Hebrew children-Shadrach, Meshach and Abed-nego are thrown into the burning fiery furnace because they refused to worship the golden image at the sound of various musical instruments. The Son of God walked in their midst in the furnace and thwarted death by incineration. In the sixth chapter of Daniel we read of how Daniel was cast into the den of lions because he continued to pray three times a day on his knees in defiance of the emperor worship that was decreed. God sent his angel and closed the mouth of the lions.

The consequence of the trials in the last two cases was that God was called as the God of Shadrach, Meshach and Abed-nego and the God of Daniel by imperial decree.

Chapter Four
Death Of Christian Believers

Precious in the sight of the LORD
is the death of his saints.
Psalm 116:15

We don't like to think about death. However, not only should we, but it is healthy that we should. It all depends on how we think about death. Do we see death as the threshold to glory? Death is the funeral of all our sorrows. We are not here to stay; we are here to go. Death never takes the wise man by surprise; He is always ready to go.

In the way of righteousness is life; and in the pathway thereof there is no death. Proverbs 12:28

When death strikes the Christian down, he falls into Heaven. Those who have welcomed Christ may welcome death. In Psalm 48:14 God is said to be our God forever and ever and our guide even unto death. God delivers the souls of the believers from the second death and keeps them alive in famine as we see in Psalm 33:19.

How pleasantly does the good man speak of dying; as if it were only a matter of going to bed! Death is never sudden to a saint; no guest comes unawares to him who keeps a constant table. The wheels of death's chariot may rattle and make a noise, but they are to carry a believer to Christ.

Death to a saint is nothing but the taking of a sweet flower out of this wilderness, and planting it in the garden of paradise. A believer's last day is his best day. Dying saints may be justly envied, while living sinners are justly pitied. The law of the wise is a fountain of life, to depart from the snares of death. Proverbs 13:14

Death is the foreshadowing of life. We die that we may die no more. Death is not so much something that happens to the Christian as something God works for him. It is no credit to your Heavenly Father for you to be reluctant to go home. While some friends were talking about death, one old lady said, "I am not looking for the undertaker, but for the Uptaker." Where you die, when you die, or by what means, is scarcely worth a thought, if you do but die in Christ.

The wicked is driven away in his wickedness: but the righteous hath hope in his death. Proverbs 14:32

How many Christians live their lives packed up and ready to go? Live so that when death comes you may embrace like friends, not encounter like enemies. Take care of your life and the Lord will take care of your death. No Christian has ever been known to recant on his deathbed.

As we face the prospect of our ministry and life's work coming to an end we kind of evaluate what we've accomplished. We look over the books, we look backward and we wonder if we've accomplished what we were supposed to accomplish and if we have left anything undone, if there's anything yet that we ought to do, and if we're going home prematurely not having accomplished all that the Lord wants us to accomplish and being called home prematurely because of failure or disobedience or stubbornness or refusal to do all that God wants us to do.

For thou hast delivered my soul from death, mine eyes from tears, and my feet from falling. Psalm 116:8

Men and women who have given themselves to God-who earnestly love and obey Him have died. They confidently declared at the portals of death, "Yea, though I walk through the valley of the shadow of death, I will fear no evil: for Thou art with me." (Psalm 23:4). He whose head is in Heaven need not fear to put his feet into the grave. The Apostle Paul said, "To die is gain" (Philippians 1:21), and "O death, where is thy sting?" (1 Corinthians 15:55).

Time of Death Can be amended by God

God is prepared to change the day of our death, if we repent for our wrongdoings. In Isaiah chapter 38, we read of the prophet Isaiah conveying the message of the Lord to King Hezekiah saying that he should set his house in order as he was to die in his sickness. Then the decree was changed when Hezekiah prayed with tears. He was granted an additional 15 years.

Death of the Righteous as 'Sleep'

In John 11.11, Jesus says: Our friend Lazarus sleeps; but I go, that I may awake him out of sleep. When Lazarus of Bethany died, Jesus said he was sleeping and then explained that he was dead. Paul speaking of those who died prematurely due to partaking unworthily in the Lord's Table: 1 Corinthians 11:30 For this cause many are weak and sickly among you, and many 'sleep'.

Dying in the faith is compared to sleeping in Jesus: 1 Thess. 4:14 For if we believe that Jesus died and rose again, even so them also which sleep in Jesus will God bring with him. Waking is compared to life in the flesh. But both states mean living with Him, as we see in 1 Thessalonians 5:10 Who died for us, that, whether we wake or sleep(dead in body), we should live together with him.

Instances of the Death of Christians

Justin Martyr, a Church father was born about 114 A.D. studied in the schools of the philosophers, searching after some knowledge that should satisfy the cravings of his soul. At last he became acquainted with Christianity, being at once impressed with the extraordinary fearlessness that the Christians displayed in the presence of death, and with the grandeur, stability, and truth of the teachings of the Old Testament. From this time he acted as an evangelist, taking every opportunity to proclaim the gospel as the only safe and certain way to salvation. While he was in Rome, the philosophers, especially the Cynics, plotted against him, and he sealed his testimony to the truth by martyrdom.

In another incident in Rome, a guard felt sorry for a Christian prisoner, who was soon to die because of his faith in Christ. He secretly allowed his daughter to visit him. After she was gone the guard stared at his prisoner. "Why do you gaze at me? "he asked. "Because you do not seem worried," was the answer. "You are to die tomorrow. Tonight you saw your daughter for the last time." "Oh, but you are wrong," exclaimed the prisoner. "I shall see her again. My daughter is a Christian, too. She will soon follow me. Christians never see one another for the last time. They meet in heaven, there to live forever. Now do you understand why I am happy and why I am ready to die for my Christian faith?"

Realizing that he would soon be gone from this world one day, Moody said to a friend, "Someday you will read in the papers that D.L. Moody of Northfield is dead. Don't you believe a word of it. At that moment I shall be more alive than I am now. I shall have gone higher, that is all out of this old clay tenement into a house that is immortal, a body that sin cannot touch, that sin cannot taint, a body fashioned like His glorious body. I was born in the flesh in 1837; I was born of the Spirit in 1856. That which is born of the flesh may die; that which is born of the Spirit will live forever."

Two contrasting views of death: An example of the first: Mark Twain, became morose and weary of life. Shortly before his death, he wrote, "A myriad of men are born; they labor and sweat and struggle;…they squabble and scold and fight; they scramble for little mean advantages over each other; age creeps upon them; infirmities follow; …those they love are taken from them, and the joy of life is turned to aching grief. It (the release) comes at last—the only unpoisoned gift earth ever had for them—and they vanish from a world where they were of no consequence,…a world which will lament them a day and forget them forever."

An example of the second in the dying words of Edward Payson: "The celestial city is full in my view. Its glories beam upon me, its breezes fan me, its odours are wafted to me, its sounds strike upon my ears, and its spirit is breathed into my heart. Nothing separates me from it but the river of death, which now appears but as an insignificant rill, that may be crossed at a single step, whenever God shall give permission. The Sun of Righteousness has been gradually drawing nearer and nearer, appearing larger and brighter as he approached, and now he fills the whole hemisphere; pouring forth a flood of glory, in which I seem to float like an insect in the beams of the sun; exulting, yet almost trembling, while I gaze on this excessive brightness, and wondering, with unutterable wonder, why God should deign thus to shine upon a sinful worm."

An elderly Christian was in much distress as he lay dying. "Oh, Pastor," he said, "for years I have relied upon the promises of God, but now in the hour of death I can't remember a single one to comfort me." Knowing that Satan was disturbing him, the preacher said, "My brother, do you think that GOD will forget any of His promises?" A smile came over the face of the dying believer as he exclaimed joyfully, "No, no! He won't! Praise the Lord, now I can fall asleep in Jesus and trust Him to remember them all and bring me safely to Heaven." Peace flooded his soul, and a short time later he was ushered by the angels into the light of God's eternal day.

When the books at God's right hand are opened, it will be revealed that some of the noblest "Giants of Faith" were men who, with only the rudiments of a formal education, lived lives that were yielded truly to Christ and wielded mightily in His service.

Polycarp was a personal disciple of the Apostle John. As an old man, he was the bishop of the Church at Smyrna in Asia Minor (present-day Turkey). Persecution against the Christians broke out there and believers were being fed to the wild beasts in the arena. The crowd began to call for the leader of the Christians- Polycarp. So the authorities sent out a search party to bring him in. They tortured two slave boys to reveal where Polycarp was being hidden.

Polycarp was resting upstairs in a country home. They came in fully armed as if they were arresting a dangerous criminal. Polycarp's friends wanted to sneak him out, but he refused, saying, "God's will be done." (The Christians there taught that a believer was not to make oneself available for martyrdom and should not seek it out, but neither should he/she avoid it when there was no choice.)

In one of the most touching instances of Christian grace imaginable, Polycarp welcomed his captors as if they were friends, talked with them and ordered that food and drink be served to them. Then Polycarp made one request: one hour to pray before they took him away. The officers overhearing his prayers (that went on for two hours) began to have second thoughts. What were they doing arresting an old man like this?

Despite the cries of the crowd; the Roman authorities saw the senselessness of making this aged man a martyr. So when Polycarp was brought into the arena, the proconsul pled with him: "Curse Christ and I will release you."

REPLY: "Eighty-six years I have served Him. He had never done me wrong. How then can I blaspheme my King who has saved me?"

The proconsul reached for an acceptable way out: "Then do this, old man. Just swear by the genius of the emperor and that will be sufficient." (The "genius" was sort of the "spirit" of the emperor. To do this would be recognition of the pagan gods and religion.)

REPLY: "If you imagine for a moment that I would do that, then I think you pretend that you don't know who I am. Hear it plainly. I am a Christian."

More entreaties. Polycarp stood firm. The proconsul threatened him with the wild beasts.

REPLY: "Bring them forth. I would change my mind if it meant going from the worse to the better, but not to change from the right to the wrong."

The proconsul's patience was gone: "I will have you burned alive."

REPLY: "You threaten fire that burns for an hour and is over. But the judgment on the ungodly is forever."

Death by fire: The fire was prepared. Polycarp lifted his eyes to heaven and prayed: "Father, I bless you that you have deemed me worthy of this day and hour, that I might take a portion of the martyrs in the cup of Christ. Among these may I today be welcome before thy face as a rich and acceptable sacrifice."

As the fire engulfed him, the believers noted that it smelled not so much like flesh burning as a loaf baking. He was finished off with the stab of a dagger. His followers gathered his remains like precious jewels and buried them on February 22, probably in the year 155. In the strange way known to the eyes of faith, it was as much a day of triumph as it was a day of tragedy.

David Livingstone, the great missionary to Africa, spoke before his death: 'All I can add in my loneliness is, May Heaven's richest blessing come down on every one — American, English, Turk — who will help to heal this open sore of the world. And the cross turns not back. The open sore will be healed. Africa will be redeemed." (Picket Line of Missions, p. 64). Livingstone was found with his head buried in his hands upon the pillow, kneeling by his bedside. At the farthest point in his journey, the soul went to its Maker, and the body remained in the attitude of prayer. Natives buried his heart in Africa, as he had requested, but his body was buried in Westminster Abbey in London.

That sweet singer, Florence Nightingale, wrote these words to Dr. Livingstone's daughter:

"He climbed the steep ascent of heaven,
 Through peril, toil, and pain;
 O God, to us may grace be given
 To follow in his train!'"

John Wesley, the day before he breathed his last broke out in verse as follows:

I'll praise my Maker while I've breath,
And when my voice is lost in death,
Praise shall employ my nobler pow'rs;
My days of praise shall ne'er be past,
While life, and thought, and being last,
Or immortality endures.

Kartar Singh, a contemporary of Sadhu Sundar Singh traveled through Punjab in India, witnessing for Jesus and finally met with martyrdom in Tibet. He was stripped of all his clothes and was sewn up in a wet yak skin, which was then put out in the sun. A cruel mocking crowd stood about to witness his tortures, and as the skin shrunk and tightened round him, they laughed to hear the bones cracking in the slow process of death.

By his side on the ground lay the New Testament that had been his one and only comfort through the hard days that had followed his confession of his Master. Unheeded it lay until on the third day, when Kartar knew the end was drawing on, he asked that his right hand might be set free for a moment. This was done, probably more from curiosity than mercy.

Collecting all his strength, Kartar wrote his last message on the flyleaf of his Testament. It was written in Urdu, which was translated into English as follows:

From God I life besought, not once but a hundred thousand times, That to what Friend again is oft I might return it. That love for Him, Khasrawa, shall not be less than hers - the faithful Hindu wife, Who on the burning pyre draws to her heart the loved one, And lays her life beside him. The life he gave to me was what I gave to Him: True it is that though I did it all, yet all I could not do.

No cry of anguish escaped the brave lips, but as evening came on, Kartar gave thanks aloud to God for comfort in death, and quietly passed away with the words, "Lord Jesus, receive my spirit".

William Carey, the consecrated cobbler, stirred a sleeping church to action and laboured valiantly in India was a remarkable example of humility and never-fading love for His Saviour:

"On one of the last occasions on which [Alexander] Duff saw him—if not the very last—he spent some time talking, chiefly about Carey's missionary life, till at length the dying man whispered 'Pray.' Duff knelt and prayed and said goodbye. As he passed from the room, he thought he heard a feeble voice pronouncing his name, and, turning, he found himself recalled. He stepped back accordingly, and this is what he heard spoken with a gracious solemnity: 'Dr. Duff, you have been speaking about Dr. Carey, Dr. Carey; when I am gone, say nothing about Dr. Carey—speak about Dr. Carey's Saviour.' Duff went away rebuked and awed, with a lesson in his heart that he never forgot"

Alexander Mackay b. 1849 d. 1890, the consecrated mechanic, endured such tears and toils in banishing the darkness of Uganda. During his last days Mackay translated the 14th chapter of John into Luganda. The words of Jesus"I go to prepare a place for you" - was the hope that cheered his lonely toiling.

Martin Luther called John 3:16 "the little gospel." When, during his last illness, someone recommended to him a certain remedy for his severe headache, he declined with these words: "The best prescription for head and heart is to be found in John 3:16." And in his dying moments he repeated the text three times.

Henry Nott, the consecrated bricklayer, who, by his heroic sufferings and unwearied labours, opened the door of Tahiti and Polynesia to the sublime tidings of a matchless text: "For God so loved the world, that he gave his only begotten Son, that whosoever believeth in him should not perish, but have everlasting life."

C.T. Studd, missionary to Africa, said: "Be sure to celebrate my funeral scripturally and send "Hallelujahs" all around. It is a better day than one's wedding day."

John Newton b. 1725. d. 1807. Originally a slaver, he had a dramatic mid-ocean change of heart that led him to turn his slave ship around and take the people back to their homeland. He became a Presbyterian minister and preached against the slave trade, inspiring William Wilberforce who brought about the abolition of slavery in Britain and its colonies.

He is famous for having authored the words to the hymn "Amazing Grace". As he neared his end, he exclaimed, "I am still in the land of the dying; I shall be in the land of the living soon."

Joseph Addison, writer, d. June 17, 1719. See in what peace a Christian can die.

Thomas à Becket, Archbishop of Canterbury, d.1170- I am ready to die for my Lord, that in my blood the Church may obtain liberty and peace.

Henry Ward Beecher, evangelist, d. March 8, 1887- Now comes the mystery.

Elizabeth Barrett Browning, writer, d. June 28, 1861- Beautiful. ~ In reply to her husband who had asked how she felt.

Thomas Alva Edison, inventor, d. October 18, 1931- It is very beautiful over there.

Edgar Allan Poe, writer, d. October 7, 1849- Lord help my poor soul.

Dr. W. B. Hinson, speaking from the pulpit a year after the commencement of the illness from which he ultimately died: "I remember a year ago when a doctor in this city said, 'You are going to die, Walt.' "I walked out to where I live, five miles out of this city, and I looked across at that mountain that I love, and I looked at the river in which I rejoice, and I looked at the stately trees that are always God's own poetry to my soul. "Then in the evening I looked up into the great sky where God was lighting his lamps, and I said: 'I may not see you many more times, but, Mountain, I shall be alive when you are gone; and, River, I shall be alive when you cease running toward the sea; and, Stars, I shall be alive when you have fallen from your sockets in the great down-pulling of the material universe!'" This is the confidence of one who knew the Saviour. Is it yours?

Selected Meditations from Morning Manna
(*The Pentecostal Mission, Chennai, India. 2005*)

Contend for the Faith
By faith, Joseph, when he died, made mention of the departing of the children of Israel; and gave commandment concerning his bones (Hebrews 11:22)

Faith gives us hope even in death. Joseph knew that one day God would visit his people and that his bones would not be in Egypt (this world), but would be carried to Canaan (heaven). This is a type of the hope of the Rapture. Even while dying, faith gives one a divine commanding authority and power. He commanded, not requested.

While dying, Joseph had a blessed hope before him of the departing of the children of Israel. In Jude verse 3, we read that we are to contend for the faith once and for all revealed to the saints of God. Joseph giving commandment concerning his bones shows how true saints should be strong to contend for the faith or doctrinal truths revealed to them.

A Better End

"Better is the end of a thing than the beginning thereof, and the patient in spirit is better than the proud in spirit" Ecclesiastes 7:8

Those who are patient in spirit will have a better end than others. We read of how patient Job was and about his end. "Behold, we count them happy which endure. Ye have heard of the patience of Job, and have seen the end of the Lord; that the Lord is very pitiful , and of tender mercy" James 5:11 Job's end was like the end of the Lord. Can anyone expect a better end than this?

Although we do not read of how Job died, his end was

like the end of the Lord, of tender mercy. The patience spoken of here is a special patience. In James 57, this patience speaks of patiently waiting for the Coming of the Lord or the Rapture. The end of such saints, whether it is their departure or the Rapture, will be better than their beginning, and rather like the end of the Lord. May the Lord grant us the grace to watch and wait patiently for His Coming.

> *"Oh, may we never weary, watching,*
> *Never lay our armour down,*
> *Until He come, and with rejoicing*
> *Give to each the promised crown."*

Pilgrims and Strangers
These all died in faith, not having received the promises, but having seen them afar off, and were persuaded of them, and embraced them, and confessed that they were strangers and pilgrims on the earth (Hebrews 11:13).

The promises referred to here were the promise of Christ and the blessings or merits of Calvary. The Old Testament saints could only see them far away by faith; but what an influence those promises had on them! They all lived confessing that they were strangers and pilgrims on the earth and died in faith. If so, how much more diligent we should be who have received the promises to live as strangers and pilgrims.

Although Abraham was a very rich man, he lived in tents and taught the tent life (faith life) to his children and grandchildren. Why? He had a revelation of a city which had foundations and whose builder and maker is God (Heb. 11:10) Obviously, that city is New Jerusalem, the city of jasper. Abraham was not called to live in the city of New Jerusalem, but when he received a revelation of the city he was able to leave his country and his kith and kin in his old age, and live in tents.

If we have faith, we will die daily; dying is gain, St. Paul says. If by faith, we can see the glorious promises of the resurrected body and of New Jerusalem and Zion, what a difference it will make to our lifestyle, easily giving up the many unnecessary things that clutter our lives!

How many things we will see as 'loss', rather than 'gain'! How many things we will throw away calling them 'dung'! How differently we would value the things we now look upon as 'dear' and 'precious'!

May the Lord help us to live in faith and die in faith- in case, the Lord tarries.

Die in Shalom

"Thou shalt come to thy grave in a full age, like as a shock of corn cometh in his season" (Job 5:26)

This is a great promise for the children of God who walk with God. A shock of corn is brought to the storehouse when it is most healthy and useful. We should not die at a time when we are useless and a burden to others, but when we are most useful and a great blessing to all (including our enemies). Read about the promise of God to Abraham: "Thou shalt go to thy fathers in peace (shalom); thou shalt be buried in a good old age". The word shalom means good health, prosperity, safety, rest, peace, completeness, etc. *"Mark the perfect man, and behold the upright: for the end of that man is peace"* (Psalm 37:7). Here also the same word shalom is used. So it is the good pleasure of God that His saints end their lives in peace- in good health, in rest, in prosperity, health prospering, the grace of God prospering and your life prospering for the glory of God.

We read that, according to God's promise, *"Abraham gave up the ghost, and died in a good old age, an old man and full of years* (Genesis 25:8). He died full of blessings, ful of gace, full of the goodness of God, full of health and full of spiritual wealth. Dear child of God, are you afraid of your future- thinking you will become sick and weak and be a burden to others? According to your faith, be it unto you. Abraham believed and God counted it as righteousness and performed what He promised to him. Let us believe as Mary did, *"Blessed is she that believed: for there shall be a performance of those things which were told her from the Lord"* (Luke 1:45). May the Lord fulfil our longing to end in peace, in shalom.

Die in Faith
"These all died in faith" (Hebrews 11:13)

Dying in faith means dying fully trusting in God, without any fear at all. Some may have a wonderful gift of faith-faith to heal the sick, raise the dead,e tc., But that faith will not help them at the time of death. We need faith as a character, faith, the fruit of the Spirit. Some people may appear bold and may seem to have great faith, but when the time comes for them to die, they are shaken. The heroes of faith stood for the faith, lived and fought for the faith, and also died for the faith.

How will you enter into your Rest?

God carefully reviews anything He does or makes. Often we do not care to do that. As God had made everything good, finally, everything was found to be very good. Finding everything that He had done to be good gave Him rest. When we realize that something we did is wrong, we are naturally restless. On the other hand, if we do everything right, we get a satisfaction and rest which we cannot get anywhere else.

Just as God entered into rest after completing His good work, after we accomplish our life-work we will enter into the rest of God. The rest will end in an endless morning (We do not see an evening on the Seventh day). Our life should end in joy- *"joy cometh in the morning"*.

The morning is fresh and beautiful. We should go to our rest in heaven with new life and joy and not with sorrow and tiredness, or with an It is enough cry as did Elijah.

We should go to rest in heaven with full satisfaction and with the joy of perfection as God did. Our works should give us full satisfaction when we enter into our rest. May our Lord be able to say to us, *"Well done, thou good and faithful servant… enter thou into the joy of the Lord."*

Blessing while Dying

"By faith Jacob, when he was a dying, blessed both the sons of Joseph; and worshipped, leaning upon the top of his staff" (Hebrews 11:21)

True saints should be a blessing, and a not a burden, even while dying. Jacob was a blessing while dying. He blessed both the sons of Joseph while dying. Faith helps us to be a blessing.

"By faith… Jacob worshipped." Faith helps us to worship the Lord in spirit and in truth till our last breath. How did Jacob worship? Jacob had the privilege and freedom to worship his God till the last moment, as Jesus did. At the time of his death, Jacob was in a heathen land with pagan gods all around, and yet he preserved his faith until death. True worshippers are truly a blessing to others till their last moment.

May the Lord grant us the grace to worship the Lord

till our last moment- if the Lord tarries and it pleases the Lord to take us to our heavenly home by death.

A life that Counts

All the days of Methuselah were nine hundred sixty and nine years; and he died.

Methuselah means *'he dies'*. It is interesting to observe that the man who lived the longest always carried death with him. It is a pity that though he lived for such a very long time on the earth, it has not been recorded that he did anything – except that he begat sons and daughters! He did not do anything for the glory of God though God had given him health and other good things.

It is not how long you live that matters, but how you live. Don't count your days, but make your days count. Let each day be your masterpiece. Invest every minute you have in things of eternal value.

Once a 17-year-old girl went to be with the Lord. Her life had been a fragrant and fruitful one and everyone was sad that she was taken away in the prime of her life. One believer asked the Lord whey He took her away so young. Then he had a vision. The girl was in heaven and one angel to another angel was introducing her. "She is 85 years old!" the angel was saying. Then the believer woke up and the Lord told him, Though physically she was only

17, spiritually she reached full age. I have completed my work in her; she has completed her life's work".

More Precious than Diamonds
Three things in life that once lost never come back: Time, Words and Opportunity.

The time that the Lord gives us here on earth is limited and most precious. To the believer and the unbeliever the word goes out from God: For it is appointed unto men once to die and then the judgment.

One late evening, a young man came upon a sack with small rocks as he walked along the seashore. He opened the sack and found in it pieces of rock. He picked up the sack and threw the stones, one by one into the seawater. At last there remained only a few small stones in the sack. When he reached home, he turned out his pocket and discovered to his great surprise that the stones were not rock pieces, but diamonds! He was extremely sad that he had thrown quite a lot of those precious stones into the depths of the sea.

Yes, all the days that have gone by were more precious than precious stones. Have you wasted your precious time in the past days? Just as the young man had a few precious stones left in his pocket, perhaps we have a few more years, a few more months or only a few more days left. Are we going to throw them also into the sea of vanity?

Let us repent for the time we have wasted in the past and use our time circumspectly, redeeming the time, knowing that the days are evil. Let us us faithfully and diligently use every moment for the glory of God, understanding the will of the Lord. May the reader who has wasted precious time have the Lord restore the years that were lost to the locust and the worm.

History of Christian Death Rites

In the world in which Christianity emerged, death was a private affair. Except when struck down on the battlefield or by accident, people died in the company of family and friends. There were no physicians or religious personnel present. Ancient physicians generally removed themselves when cases became hopeless. Priests and priestesses served their gods rather than ordinary people.

Contact with a corpse caused ritual impurity and hence ritual activity around the deathbed was minimal. A relative might bestow a final kiss or attempt to catch a dying person's last breath. The living closed the eyes and mouth of the deceased. They then washed the corpse, anointed it with scented oil and herbs, and dressed it, sometimes in clothing befitting the social status of the deceased, sometimes in a shroud.

A procession accompanied the body to the necropolis

outside the city walls. There it was laid to rest, or cremated and given an urn burial, in a family plot that often contained a structure to house the dead.

Beyond such more or less shared features, funeral rites, as well as forms of burial and commemoration, varied as much as the people and the ecology of the region in which Christianity developed and spread. Cremation was the common mode of disposal in the Roman Empire. Older patterns of corpse burial persisted in Egypt and the Middle East. Christianity arose among Jews, who buried their dead.

Although Christians practiced inhumation (corpse burial) from the earliest times, they were not, as often assumed, responsible for the gradual disappearance of cremation in the Roman Empire during the second and third centuries, for common practice was already changing before Christianity became a major cultural force. However, Christianity was, in this case, in sync with wider patterns of cultural change. Hope of salvation and attention to the fate of the body and the soul after death were more or less common features of all the major religious movements of the age, including the Hellenistic mysteries, Christianity, Rabbinic Judaism, Manichaeanism, and Mahayana Buddhism, which was preached as far west as Alexandria.

Early Christian Responses to Death and Dying

Early Christians were slow to develop specifically Christian responses to death and dying. Christians handled the bodies of the dead without fear of pollution. The Christian living had less need than their neighbours to appease their dead, who were not likely to return as unhappy ghosts. Non-Christians noted the joyous mood at Christian funerals and the ease of the participants in the presence of the dead. Christians gave decent burials to even the poorest of the poor.

Chapter Five
Death Of Unbelievers

Then when lust hath conceived, it brings forth sin: and sin,
when it is finished, brings forth death.
James 1:15

Fear of Death

The fear of doom is part of the judgments of God on the guilty and those who seek to hide sin, "who through fear of death were all their lifetime subject to bondage." (Hebrews 2:15). In Ecclesiastes 8:8 , we read that "There is no man that hath power over the spirit to retain the spirit; neither hath he power in the day of death: and there is no discharge in that war; neither shall wickedness deliver those that are given to it."

The author of this book was himself a daredevil in the days of his youth sitting on the window ledge of express trains with the arms, legs and head jutting out of the window. One fall would have meant certain death. And yet the sinful, have an evil fascination for death! That's why they ride these motorcycles at breakneck speed and love the fast car races and dangerous sports, anything that dares death, defies death, these stunt men doing death-defying stunts, dangerous mountain climbs and dangerous feats of all kinds. It reminds us of that Scripture: "Them that love death!" (Proverbs 8:36).

They are fascinated by death! They act like they really want to die, like they're daring the Devil to kill them! But when it comes right down to it, then they don't want to! To so many people death is a fearsome, dreadful thing. Let us visit the deathbeds of the unbelievers.

Aristotle wrote: "Death is a dreadful thing, for it is the end!"

Thomas Hobbes, writer, who died in 1679 said: "I am about to take my last voyage, a great leap in the dark."

John Donne, the English author, wrote: "Death is a bloody conflict and no victory at last; a tempestuous sea, and no harbor at last; a slippery height and no footing; a desperate fall and no bottom!"

Rousseau cried, "No man dares to face death without fear."

Churchill: English Statesman and co-conspirator of the selling out of Eastern Europe at Yalta to Russia & Communism, together with fellow Freemasons Roosevelt and Stalin, wrote in his autobiography: "I could have prevented the war!" (W.W.II). He said at his deathbed: "What a fool I have been!"

David Hume, the atheist, cried: "I am in flames!" His desperation was a horrible scene.

Sir Thomas Scott, once president of the English Lower House said: "Up until this time, I thought that there was no God neither Hell. Now I know and feel that there are both, and I am delivered to perdition by the righteous judgment of the Almighty."

Karl Marx, born in a Christian Jewish family, originator of Communism. On his deathbed surrounded by candles burning to Lucifer, screamed at his nurse who asked him if he had any last words: "Go on, get out! Last words are for fools who haven't said enough."

Friedrich Nietzsche, pernicious philosopher who preached "God is dead" Nietzsche died in spiritual darkness, a babbling madman. On a wall in Austria a graffiti said, "God is dead, --Nietzsche!" Someone else wrote under it, "Nietzsche is dead! --God."

The infidel, Robert Ingersoll, when standing at the grave of his brother, said, "Life is a narrow vale between the cold and barren peaks of two eternities. We strive in vain to look beyond the height. We cry aloud, and the only answer is the echo of our wailing cry. From the voiceless lips of the unreplying dead there comes no word."

After the death of Alexander the Great one of his

generals, Ptolemy Philadelphus, inherited Egypt and lived a selfish life amid wealth and luxury. As he grew old, he was haunted by the fear of death, and even sought in the lore of Egyptian priests the secret of eternal life. One day, seeing a beggar lying content in the sun, Ptolemy said, "Alas, that I was not born one of these!"

Honore Mirabeau, a leading political organizer of the French Revolution: "My sufferings are intolerable: I have in me a hundred years of life, but not a moment's courage. Give me more laudanum that I may not think of eternity! O Christ, O Jesus Christ!"

Mazarin, French cardinal and advisor to kings: "O my poor soul! What will become of thee? Wither wilt thou go?"

Severus, Roman emperor who caused the death of thousands of Christians: "I have been everything; and everything is nothing!"

Thomas Hobbes, the political philosopher and sceptic who corrupted some of England's great men: "If I had the whole world, I would give anything to live one day. I shall be glad to find a hole to creep out of the world at. I am about to take a fearful leap in the dark!"

Caesar Borgia: "I have provided, in the course of my life, for everything except death; and now, alas! I am to die, although entirely unprepared!"

Sir Thomas Scott, chancellor of England: "Until this

moment, I thought there was neither God nor hell; now I know and feel that there are both, and I am doomed to perdition by the just judgment of the Almighty!"

Edward Gibbon, author of "Decline and Fall of the Roman Empire": "All is dark and doubtful!"

Sir Francis Newport, the head of an English infidel club to those gathered around his deathbed: "You need not tell me there is no God for I know there is one, and that I am in His presence! You need not tell me there is no hell. I feel myself already slipping. Wretches, cease your idle talk about there being hope for me! I know I am lost forever! Oh, that fire! Oh, the insufferable pangs of hell!"

M.F. Rich: "Terrible horrors hang over my soul! I have given my immortality for gold; and its weight sinks me into a hopeless, helpless Hell!"

Thomas Paine, the leading atheistic writer in American colonies: "I would give worlds if I had them, that The Age of Reason had never been published. O Lord, help me! Christ, help me! . . No, don't leave; stay with me! Send even a child to stay with me; for I am on the edge of Hell here alone. If ever the Devil had an agent, I have been that one."

Aldamont, the infidel: "My principles have poisoned my friend; my extravagance has beggared my boy; my unkindness has murdered my wife. And is there another hell yet ahead?"

John Wilkes Booth, who assassinated Abraham Lincoln: "Useless! Useless! The terrors before me!"

Thomas Carlyle: "I am as good as without hope; a sad old man gazing into the final chasm."

David Strauss, leading representative of German rationalism, after spending a lifetime erasing belief in God from the minds of others: "My philosophy leaves me utterly forlorn! I feel like one caught in the merciless jaws of an automatic machine, not knowing at what time one of its great hammers may crush me!"

John Lennon: Some years before during his interview with an American Magazine, he said: "Christianity will end, it will disappear. I do not have to argue about that. I am certain. Jesus was ok, but his subjects were too simple, today we are more famous than Him" (1966)". Lennon, after saying that the Beatles were more famous than Jesus Christ, was shot six times.

Tancredo Neves, a Brazilian banker and politician during the Presidential campaign, said if he got 500 votes from his party, not even God would remove him from Presidency. Sure he got the votes, but just one day before he was scheduled to take the oath of office (March 15, 1985), Neves became severely ill. He suffered from abdominal complications and developed generalized infections. After seven operations, Tancredo Neves died on April 21, 1985.

Cazuza, a Brazilian composer, singer and poet. During a show in Canecão (Rio de Janeiro), whilst smoking his cigarette, he puffed out some smoke into the air and said: God, that's for you. He died in Rio de Janeiro in 1990 at the age of 32 due to AIDS related illness.

The man who built the Cruise Liner Titanic, in an ironic tone replied a reporter who queried about the safety of the Titanic: "Not even God can sink it."

On April 10, 1912, the RMS Titanic set sail from Southampton on her maiden voyage to New York. At that time, she was the largest and most luxurious ship ever built. At 11:40 PM on April 14, 1912, she struck an iceberg about 400 miles off Newfoundland, Canada. Less than three hours later, the Titanic plunged to the bottom of the sea, taking more than 1500 people with her. Only a fraction of her passengers were saved.

Marilyn Monroe: Billy Graham visited her, during a presentation of a show. He is a preacher and Evangelist and the Spirit of God had sent him to preach to her.

After hearing what the Preacher had to say, she said: "I don't need your Jesus." A week later, she was found dead in her apartment.

Christine Hewitt, a Jamaican Journalist and entertainer, said the Bible (Word of God) was the worst book ever written. In June 2006, she was found burnt beyond recognition in her motor vehicle.

Bon Scott, the ex-vocalist of the AC/DC On one of his 1979 songs he sang: "Don't stop me, I'm going down all the way, wow the highway to hell". On the 19th of February 1980, Bon Scott was found dead; he had been choked by his vomit.

CAMPINAS/SP IN 2005: In Campinas, Brazil, a group of friends, drunk, went to pick up a friend. The mother accompanied her to the car and was so worried about the drunkenness of her friends and she said to the daughter-holding her hand, who was already seated in the car: "MY DAUGHTER, GO WITH GOD AND MAY HE PROTECT YOU."

She responded: "ONLY IF HE (GOD) TRAVELS IN THE BOOT, COZ INSIDE HERE IT'S ALREADY FULL." Hours later, news came by that they had been involved in a fatal accident; everyone had died. The car could not be recognized, but surprisingly, the boot was intact. The police said there was no way the boot could have remained intact. To their surprise, inside the boot was a crate of eggs-none was broken.

Billionaire Ken Hendricks built his company, ABC Supply, into a giant with annual sales of nearly $3 billion. In 2004, Ken said: "We didn't invent anything. But even Jesus Christ had a roof, and it probably had to be repaired,". He died tragically in December 2007, while working on his garage roof. It collapsed and he suffered a fatal head injury.

Leona Helmsley, American hotel heiress and

billionaire died at age 87, posthumously leaving her dog $12 million.

Death of Autocrats and Tyrants

Charles IX was the French king who, urged on by his mother, gave the order for the massacre of the Huguenots, in which 15,000 souls were slaughtered in Paris alone and 100,000 in other sections of France, for no other reason than that they loved Christ. The guilty king suffered miserably for years after that event. He finally died, bathed in blood bursting from his veins. To his physicians he said in his last hours:

"Asleep or awake, I see the mangled forms of the Huguenots passing before me. They drop with blood. They point at their open wounds. Oh! that I had spared at least the little infants at the breast! What blood! I know not where I am. How will all this end? What shall I do? I am lost forever! I know it. Oh, I have done wrong."

Napoleon Bonaparte, the French emperor who brought death to millions to satisfy his selfish plans: "I die before my time, and my body will be given back to the earth. Such is the fate of him who has been called the great Napoleon. What an abyss between my deep misery and the eternal kingdom of Christ!"

Tallyrand was one of the most cunning French political leaders of the Napoleonic era. On a paper found at his death were these words: "Behold eighty-three passed away! What cares! What agitation! What anxieties! What ill will! What sad complications! And all without other results except great fatigue of mind and body, a profound sentiment of discouragement with regard to the future, and disgust with regard to the past!"

Vladimir Il'ich Lenin, architect of the October Revolution and the "leader of the world's proletariat," died on January 21, 1924 succumbing to complications from three strokes. The cult of Lenin was a fusion of political and religious ritual, inspired by both genuine reverence and a political desire to mobilize the masses. The Politburo, against the wishes of Lenin and of his family, embalmed his body and placed it in a sarcophagus inside a cube-like mausoleum of gleaming red granite on Red Square.

Here, the most prominent party, military and government leaders would stand to view parades passing by on the anniversary of the October Revolution, May Day and other special occasions. Within the party itself, Lenin was revered in a demigod fashion with the slogan "Lenin lived, Lenin lives, Lenin will live".

Mussolini, the Italian dictator, was captured by Italian partisans, executed, then hung upside down and thrown into the gutter.

Hitler and Goebbels: The day before his death, Hitler "raged like a madman" with a ferocity never seen before.

With the desertions of Göring and Himmler and the Soviets advancing deep into Berlin, Hitler began preparing for his own death. On 28 April 1945 he dictated his last will and a two-part political testament. He essentially blamed the Jews for everything, including the Second World War. He also made a reference to his 1939 threat against the Jews along with a veiled reference to the subsequent gas chambers.

……….. Above all I charge the leaders of the nation and those under them to scrupulous observance of the laws of race and to merciless opposition to the universal poisoner of all peoples, International Jewry.

-Adolf Hitler, Berlin, this 29th day of April 1945, 4:00A.M.

Hitler thought that death would be a release for him after the recent betrayal of his oldest friends and supporters. Hitler had his poison tested on his favorite dog, Blondi and handed poison capsules to his secretaries while apologizing that he did not have better parting gifts to give them. The capsules were for them to use if the Soviets stormed the bunker. The body of Hitler was found sprawled on the sofa, dripping with blood from a gunshot to his right temple. Eva Braun had died from swallowing poison.

As Soviet shells exploded nearby, the bodies were carried up to the Chancellery garden, doused with gasoline and burned while Bormann and Goebbels stood by and gave a final Nazi salute. Over the next three hours the bodies were repeatedly doused with gasoline. The charred remains were then swept into a canvas, placed into a shell crater and buried. On the following day, May 1, Goebbels and his wife proceeded to poison their six young children in a bunker and were shot in the back of the head by an SS man. Their bodies were then burned, but were only partially destroyed and were not buried.

Stalin, the tyrant who brought about the death of millions of his own people through famine and purges, died at 73, after 30 years of despotic rule of the Soviet Union. Despite this, 500 people lost their lives trying to get a glimpse of the corpse. In a Newsweek interview with Svetlana Stalin, the daughter of Josef Stalin, told of her father's death: "My father died a difficult and terrible death. God grants an easy death only to the just.

At what seemed the very last moment he suddenly opened his eyes and cast a glance over everyone in the room. It was a terrible glance, insane or perhaps angry. . His left hand was raised, as though he were pointing to something above and bringing down a curse on us all. The gesture was full of menace. The next moment he was dead."

SUICIDES

William E. Henley, an atheist, wrote a famous poem, the last two lines of which have often been quoted:

"And yet the menace of the years
Finds, and shall find, me unafraid.
It matters not how strait the gate,
How charged with punishment the scroll,
I am the master of my fate;
I am the captain of my soul."

Men who have been bold in their defiance of God have lauded Henley's poem, but most of them were not aware that Henley later committed suicide.

George Davey Smith reports that premature deaths in Hollywood is often the mixture of drugs, drink, sex, violence, monstrous egos, gangsterism, speed, and madness of sometimes has-been) stars. The suicides are indicative of the roller coaster nature of fame: Albert Dekker wrote sections of the poor reviews from his last film in crimson lipstick on his body before hanging himself; Lou Tellegen stabbed himself with gold scissors engraved with his name, surrounded by film posters, photographs, and newspaper cuttings from his days of triumph.

Peg Enwistle jumped to her death from one of the giant letters of the Hollywood sign (setting off a spate of copycat leaps into oblivion). Among the better known suicides are Marilyn Monroe and her Oscar-winning co-star in All About Eve, George Sanders, whose note read "Dear World: I am leaving you because I am bored. I am leaving you with your worries in this sweet cesspool."

To these suicides can be added the long list of those for whom the road to excess led to premature demise. Among the stars of the silent screen were Wally Reid (morphine), John Gilbert (drink), Alma Rubens (heroin), Olive Thomas (barbiturates), Marie Prevost (drink), and Barbara La Marr (everything).

The overdose at 50 of Don Simpson—Hollywood actor and producer, encapsulates the idea that it is better to burn out than to fade away. With his $60 000 a month drug habit, orgies, fights, and busts, it was said that "Don was never afraid of getting old. He was afraid of getting fat. He died at a remarkably old age, given the way he was living."

Death of Voltaire French author, humanist, rationalist (1694–1778). The most influential atheist of Europe in his day, held up a copy of the Bible in the air and smugly proclaimed, "In 100 years this book will be forgotten and eliminated...".

Voltaire cried out with his dying breath: "I am abandoned by God and man; I shall go to hell! I will give you half of what I am worth, if you will give me six months life." Shortly after his death, Voltaire's private residence became the home of the Geneva Bible Society and his printing presses were used to print thousands of Bibles. The Christian physician who attended Voltaire during his last illness later wrote about the experience:

"When I compare the death of a righteous man, which is like the close of a beautiful day, with that of Voltaire, I see the difference between bright, serene weather and a black thunderstorm. Often did I tell him the truth. 'Yes, my friend,' he would often say to me, 'you are the only one who has given me good advice. Had I but followed it, I should not be in the horrible condition in which I now am. I have swallowed nothing but smoke. I have intoxicated myself with the incense that turned my head. You can do nothing for me. Send me an insane doctor! Have compassion on me! I am mad!'

"I cannot think of it without shuddering. As soon as he saw that all the means he had employed to increase his strength had just the opposite effect death was constantly before his eyes. From this moment, madness took possession of his soul. He expired under the torments of the furies."

The death of King Saul
King Saul was sore wounded of the archers and he knew he was dying, and yet, instead of using the last few moments to repent and prepare for his eternity, he was still seeking dignity and honour. *"Then said Saul unto his armourbearer, draw thy sword, and thrust me through therewith; lest these uncircumcised Philistines come and thrust me through and*

abuse me.." (I Samuel 31:4). Obviously, he did not want anybody to say after his death that he had been killed by an uncircumcised person. Whoever it was who killed him, he was going to go to hell; but that appeared to be his least concern!

The armourbearer refused to kill him. Saul took a sword and fell on it. But his suicidal attempt failed. He realized that even death was hating him. Then Saul saw an Amalekite and requested him to kill him. The Amalekite stood upon him and cut off his head. In what a pathetic backslidden state he ended his life!

Saul's end is a warning to every one of us. It proves how pride can make our life and death and eternity most miserable. Saul did not want an uncircumcised Philistine to kill him, but what a disgrace it was to have to ask an Amalekite- the Amalekites were worse and more abominable than the Philistines- to kill him. The honour of this world is like a shadow- the more we follow it, the more it flees from us.

Dear Unbeliever, When you Die…
The thief cometh not, but for to steal, and to kill, and to destroy: I am come that they might have life, and that they might have it more abundantly" (John 10:10)

Many years ago, in East Surrey Hospital, London, a lady, Mrs. Burgess, lay dying. The bed next to her was occupied by another lady named Joan Plumridge who was also very sick. One night Joan saw a demon with two horns enter by the main gate of the hospital and come straight to Mrs.Burgess and even as she looked on, she saw the demon carry her away. Mrs.Burgess screamed loudly and the next moment she was dead. That very moment, Joan Plumridge who was a drunkard was convicted of her sins and she committed her life to Christ. Later on, she became a wonderful servant of God and led hundreds of souls to Christ.

"The thief cometh not, but for to steal and to kill and to destroy". Yes, first the devil, the thief, steals peace, joy and grace out of our lives. Finally, he steals our very soul. However, Jesus came to give us life and abundant life.

If you die today, where will you spend your eternity? Will Jesus and the angels come and carry you to heaven or will the devil carry you to hellfire? Choose to follow Christ. He is our life and peace. Your decision will determine your destiny.

How to Preach at a Funeral
(for someone you suspect died unsaved)

by Mike Smalley
Source: How to live forever without being religious. By Ray Comfort, 2006

1. Start in the natural realm and move into the spiritual realm.
2. Say something positive about the person
3. Don't feel pressured to say anything about where the deceased may have gone after death. God only knows.
4. Never suggest that the deceased went to Heaven.
5. Mention that the death reminds us that we shall all die and that we must make preparations for that day.
6. Use anecdotes that convey eternal truth.
7. Go quickly through each of the Ten Commandments.
8. Warn briefly about sin, death, judgment and eternity.
9. Give a clear Gospel presentation.
10. Appeal to hearers to repent today.

When anyone dies, I ask myself: Was I faithful? Did I speak all the truth? And did I speak it from my very soul every time I preached? – Charles Spurgeon.

Let us close this chapter with the quote below:
Say unto them, As I live, saith the Lord GOD, I have no pleasure in the death of the wicked; but that the wicked turn from his way and live: turn ye, turn ye from your evil ways; for why will ye die, O house of Israel? Ezekiel 33:11.

Chapter Six
First Adam: First Death

*Wherefore, as by one man sin entered into the world,
and death by sin; and so death passed upon all men,
for that all have sinned:*
Romans 5:12

Adam, the first man was created as a minuscule and limited or finite, replica of the image of the uncreated, undying Infinite Triune God. Adam was created with body, soul and spirit, all of which were charged with eternal life, glory and immortality.

Though immortal, Adam could die; sinless, but could sin; had free will; was holy, loving, gentle, kind, good, meek and humble, among other godly virtues, as the Blessed God is, as the Lord Jesus is and the holy angels are.

When Eve, the first woman, taken out of the side of Adam, was deceived by Satan (the Serpent) and when Adam disobeyed God, in obeying the wicked suggestion of his wife, the entire physical creation, plunged into spiritual death, vanity, darkness, chaos and rebellion. Spiritual and bodily death came to all due to the disobedience of one man.

Death as a phenomenal power, under Satan, took force in creation. However, God Almighty, the Creator of physical and spiritual Life, has always had overall sovereign power over death. Elijah and Enoch have until this day, been free from the power of death.

Satan, as the Instigator, and Adam and Eve as co-operating agents all received their judgment. Billions of human souls, the seed of Adam, have inherited the nature of sin, since the Fall of Adam.

Ever since he fell in the Eternity that preceded the creation of the earth and Adam, Satan- that great Serpent, had actually, already been condemned to be tormented in the Lake of Fire forever.

The bruising of the head of the Serpent by the seed of the woman, as predicted by God, has already taken place, when Jesus- The Son of God, yet the seed of Eve, through Mary, crushed the head of Satan on Calvary, and we i.e., our sins and Satan bruised the feet of Jesus. However, Satan operates through his lies and the power of sin in the fallen flesh of man.

He has ever since, been working night and day to drag as many souls with him to Hell as possible.

FIRST DEATH

Spiritual Death

The first death consisted of a spiritual alienation from the life of God in the soul and spirit, as well as the power of death entering the previously immortal body of man. Darkness and death entered the spirit and soul of Adam, the moment he disobeyed God. Physical death (of the body) came only 930 years later for Adam, clearly showing the waning effects of the immortality on the fallen flesh of man. The life span of fallen man was more than ten times longer than today and it diminished rapidly after the Flood.

Fallen man in the process of reproduction transmitted the power of sin and death- spiritual as well as physical death, to all succeeding generations. Thus, through one man's disobedience, biological reproduction of man or the proliferation of human life, innately implied the proliferation of human souls involuntarily brought under the power of sin and death. This power sprouts from the soul, with and without evil influences from outside, in all the children of men.

The power of death, decay and degeneration has ever since become only greater and the span of life become shorter and shorter.

Law of Sin and (Spiritual) Death

The law of sin and (spiritual) death operates in all unbelievers, as well as Christians who do not enter into the domain of the law of the Spirit and an endless life in Christ Jesus. Paul reports this experience of bondage to the law of sin operating in his members in Romans chapter seven.

Nakedness- First outcome of Spiritual Death

The loss of immortality and the glory of God that covered Adam and Eve were accompanied by the appearance of spiritual death and the power of mortality and corruption. Satan stripped Adam and Eve of their innocence and clothing of the garments of glory. The shame of nakedness was consequent to disobeying God and yielding to Satan. Ever since, Satan has always attempted to worsen the plight of men and women, despite the extricate arts and vanities of weaving and fashion.

Fallen man is painfully ignorant of the basic truth that man is the only creature that uses clothes to cover nakedness. Another truth, equally remarkable, is that man without proper spiritual covering, even with elaborate clothing, feels naked unto himself, before God, and his fellow men.

Jesus as the Sinless Lamb of God was the first man, after Adam fell, to appear in sinless flesh in the likeness

or disguise of the appearance of fallen ma
have been partaker of the utter wretchedn
Cross of Calvary, after the soldiers cast ⌐
When Jesus rose from the dead, the gr
tomb and He appeared clothed with
of holiness and righteousness. Fai
the blood of Christ is the only wa
children can be clothed again b

Prenatal and Postnatal Life
The first phase of life insi
marked by rapid growth
with the nutrients supp
conception itself is in
    The second pha
copious consumpti
ungodly and the ·
with no land, n
physical death
men, out of
provide an
    It is
miserab⌐
who ce
let al
gra

portrayed as the representative of this class of the poorest, most oppressed and utterly destitute souls of men. He was so helpless that he could not keep the dogs away from feeding on the inflamed and pus-filled, sores of his body, let alone worship on the Sabbath day in the synagogue or the temple.

Spiritual death and Eternal Life contrasted
Death came through the first Adamic disobedience, but fruit unto death is also generated through the motions of sins working in the members of the body (Rom.7.5). It is death to be carnally minded, while the spiritually minded have life and peace (Rom. 8.6). The carnal mind is called enmity against God, even as death is called as the last enemy that will be defeated.

We read of some pseudo-christians who are considered twice dead in "Jude 1:12 These are spots in your feasts of charity, when they feast with you, feeding themselves without fear: clouds they are without water, carried about of winds; trees whose fruit withereth, without fruit, twice dead, plucked up by the roots." This may be referring to death in the soul and spirit, though the body was physically alive.

Salvation in the Christian experience is one of passing from death to life (John 5.24). Not loving the fellow man or brother is compared to abiding in death and darkness (I

John 3.14,15). Hating the brother is compared to murder. Jesus speaking to the angel of the church in Sardis says: "....I know thy works, that thou hast a name that thou livest, and art dead (Rev. 3:1), implying that nominal Christians are spiritually dead.

Eternal Life is compared to light (Matt.6.22), both in the form of the eyes of the body functioning as the lamp giving light to the whole being, as well as the good works of the Christian shining in the darkness of this world to bring glory to the Father (Matt. 5.16).

The prophet speaks in Isa 38:17...but thou hast in love to my soul delivered it from the pit of corruption and Paul declares boldly that he is persuaded "...that neither death, nor life, nor angels, nor principalities, nor powers, nor things present, nor things to come can separate us from the love of God in Christ Jesus our Lord (Rom. 8.38,39).

Death as a Power

Considering the verse below, we can understand that Death and Hell (Hades) follow each other and that both are depicted here as real powers.

Rev. 6:8 And I looked, and behold a pale horse: and his name that sat on him was Death, and Hell followed with him. And power was given unto them over the fourth part of the earth, to kill with sword, and with hunger, and with death, and with the beasts of the earth.

Death as a Location

The souls of the dead are located according to the verse below in 3 different places: the sea, death and hell (Hades).

Revelation 20:13 And the sea gave up the dead which were in it; and death and hell delivered up the dead which were in them: and they were judged every man according to their works.

And yet again, we read that the contents of death and hell (Hades) were cast into the lake of fire that is the place and power of the Second Death.

Death as Power exercised by God

Satan is not the absolute dispenser of death. The devil's power is subject to the overruling by God who could exercise the power of death at His Own Sovereign Discretion. In Ex 12:29, we read ….., that at midnight the LORD smote all the firstborn in the land of Egypt, from the firstborn of Pharaoh that sat on his throne unto the firstborn of the captive that was in the dungeon; and all the firstborn of cattle.

Nadab and Abihu- sons of Aaron, the families of Korah and Dathan, and the thousands who died following the plague and the serpents in the wilderness were direct consequences of God's judgment.

Unusual Deaths
Death of people due to suicide, homicide, ' natural' disasters and 'accidents' may or may not be due to divine judgment. The Bible does not approve of suicide. God rejected Saul, Samson was a captive of his enemies and Judas Iscariot betrayed Jesus before their respective, tragic, suicidal deaths.

Some so-called Christians are foolish enough to claim God's revenge through the sudden, early deaths of their enemies or dissenters. Some others resort to invoking curses, judgment unto death, or punishment and so forth. Jesus rebuked the disciples when they wanted Him to bring down fire upon the Samaritans who refused to receive Jesus.

He told those who reported about the 18 deaths caused by the collapse of the tower in Siloam that they should not think that …they were sinners above all men that dwelt in Jerusalem? (Luke 13:4). He also told those who reported about Pilate mixing the blood of Galileans in the sacrifice of the Jews that they should not "…Suppose .. that these Galilaeans were sinners above all the Galilaeans, because they suffered such things? (Luke 13:2).

Judgment of the body to redeem the spirit
Saint Paul suggested that the Corinthian fornicator should be delivered "….unto Satan for the destruction of the

flesh, that the spirit may be saved in the day of the Lord Jesus (1Cor 5:5). Paul also refers to "…Hymenaeus and Alexander; whom I have delivered unto Satan, that they may learn not to blaspheme (1Tim. 1:20) probably for the death of their bodies, for the purpose of redemption of their spirit and soul on the Day of Christ.

Chapter Seven
Last Adam: Eternal Life

For if by one man's (Adam's) offence death reigned by one;
much more they which receive abundance of grace and of the
gift of righteousness shall reign in life
by one, Jesus Christ.
Romans 5:17

Jesus Christ- The Last Adam

The first Adam was created sinless, but died in his sin,
though with the hope of the Redeemer. Jesus is the Second
and Last Adam, the Prince of Life (Acts3.15). As we read
in I Corinthians 15.47,. the first man was of the earth,
earthy, the second Man is the Lord from Heaven. Jesus-
the Son of God, incarnated without sin, as the seed of Eve,
through the virgin Mary, lived without sin and finally,
died on the cross without sin. Christ is the Lord both of
the dead and living.

Verily, verily, I say unto you, He that hears my word,

and believeth on him that sent me, hath everlasting life, and shall not come into condemnation; but is passed from death unto life. John 5:24

Those who hear the words of Jesus (or read) and believe that He spoke the Words of Life will receive forgiveness and life. Verily, verily, I say unto you, If a man keep my saying, he shall never see death. John 8:51 Faith in Christ is the keeping of the words of Jesus and translation of His commands into our life.

Jesus challenged the Jews to kill his body and declared that He would raise up His own body (referring to it as a temple greater than the temple of Herod) in three days. And He did just that. Paul says: "Knowing that Christ being raised from the dead dies no more; death has no more dominion over him" (Rom. 6:9).

After a life of prayer, sufferings and daily carrying of the cross of rejection, the Lord Jesus Christ, died on the Cross making eternal Life available to all men through faith. Jesus Christ brought His own sinless flesh and blood as a sin offering. The sinless lifeblood of The Last Adam-the Lord from Heaven, was poured out in a sacrifice mediated at Calvary by the Blessed Holy Spirit.

Through His Atoning Death, the Lord Jesus abolished spiritual death and brought life and immortality to light in his human frame for the benefit of all mankind. The first death continued/s in the lives of unbelievers and those believers who would not understand what Jesus meant when He said: He that liveth and believeth in me shall never die ! Because Jesus knew that He would offer His own body to die to sin once for all (Rom.6.10). In Psalm 68:20 we read that unto God belong the issues of death. The issues of death belong to the God of our salvation who delivers souls from death.

Christ, as the Root and Offspring of David, has with Him the keys of Hell (Hades) and Death. Thus, the mediator between God and man, the man Christ Jesus, as the sinless Agent of Eternal life and Atonement, is seated on the very Throne of the Father. Hallelujah!

Heart of the Earth- Place of the dead
In Matthew 12:40, we read that "..as Jonas was three days and three nights in the whale's belly; so shall the Son of man be three days and three nights in the heart of the earth." The term is clearly referring to a spiritual dimension located in the centre of the physical planet earth. Jesus was among the righteous dead souls and the souls of the people physically judged by the worldwide deluge, preaching the gospel personally to them, in a period of existence that in our dimension meant three days and nights.

Eternal Life
The people that walked in darkness have seen a great light:

they that dwell in the land of the shadow of death, upon them hath the light shined. Isaiah 9:2

Read also Psalm 102:20, Psalm 107:9-14; Matthew 4:16; Luke 1:79.

An altogether new kind of life, also called 'eternal life', commences when the sinner under conviction of sin, confesses the faith of his heart that Jesus died on the Cross for him and lives to justify him. Eternal life has a beginning for the believer, but has no end. The death of the body does not even set a punctuation mark on the course of this eternal life.

It is the gaining of what Adam lost in the spiritual dimension of the heart and soul, by literally receiving the Spirit of Jesus by faith into one's heart and life.

In Romans 8:1-2, Paul celebrates the law of the spirit of life in Christ Jesus that set him free from the law of sin and death.

While the character of eternal life is heavenly, the character of pain, sickness and weakness are all the result of the spiritual death. It is hellish and bears all the hallmarks of the separation of sinful man from the goodness of God. While the seed of death is implanted in all men, since Adam, through reproduction, the seed of eternal life is implanted into the heart/soul by a new spiritual birth that enables one to see Jesus as the Messiah or the Christ, and not just another wise human teacher or philosopher.

In 2 Timothy 1:10, we read that Our Saviour has abolished death and brought life and immortality to light through the gospel. The incorruptible seed of eternal life is to be nourished by the Word of God, the Holy Spirit, and fellowship with other Christians and abiding in the death of Christ whereunto the believer was initially immersed at water baptism. The well of life that Jesus promised the Samaritan woman at Jacob's well, becomes a fountain springing up and becoming rivers of living water that gush out from the belly of the believer.

End of faith or salvation of the soul

This life, like the fragile life of an infant, whose senses and immune system are not sufficiently strong and well-developed, may be poisoned or even killed by undue fellowship with unbelievers, the world, sin, the fleshly lusts of the believer and Satan. It is believed that if such a person dies without being reconciled to God, the backslider will find himself in outer darkness and outside the city of God. Rev.22.15.

'Once saved, always saved' is a doctrine that should be challenged, as the eternal life and salvation imparted at the new birth is consolidated and finally secured, only in leaving this world in the faith, in sleeping into the Lord or at the Rapture. As Paul writes: Receiving the end of your faith, even the salvation of your souls.

Death of Death in the Death of Christ
Death stung himself to death when he stung Christ.

The Son of God found Himself in the form of a man we read in Philippians 2:8 and as though that humbling was not enough, he became obedient unto death, even the death of the cross. The bodily death of Christ was preceded by numerous nights of intense prayer from His Soul with many tears for mankind as stated in Hebrews 5:7 "Who in the days of his flesh, when he had offered up prayers and supplications with strong crying and tears unto him that was able to save him from death, and was heard in that he feared;". This led up finally to the agonizing prayer in the garden at Gethsemane when the travail of His soul led to His sinless Blood flowing through sweat pores. Jesus told his disciples in Mark 14:34 My soul is exceeding sorrowful unto death: tarry ye here, and watch.

In Proverbs 16:14 it is written that the wrath of a king is as messengers of death, but a wise man will pacify it. Jesus is the Wise Man who pacified the Wrath of God-The Father, The King, whose anger came upon Jesus on the Cross. Faith in His Atoning Death releases the soul of the believer from the Wrath of God- the Second Death or the Lake of Fire.

The back of The Christ of God was ripped to shreds by the cruel whipping with the bone-decorated cat of nine tails. The back of the Son of God was like a well-ploughed field. The rod of the anger of the Holy and Just God- The Father, came upon my King who opened not His mouth like a sheep before His shearers. Carrying the cruellest weapon of execution ever invented, this Amazing Love in Flesh and Blood walked in full awareness of the purpose of His Eternal Mission- namely, to destroy him who had the power of death- physical, spiritual and eternal death.

My God, my God why have You forsaken me!
Psalm 22:1; Matthew 27:46; Mark 15:34

As recorded in Hebrews 2:9, Christians see Jesus who was made a little lower than the angels for the suffering of death, crowned with glory and honour; that he by the grace of God should taste death for every man. The Creator Lord humbled Himself to partake of the created form of flesh and blood (See Hebrews 2:14) so that through death He might destroy him that had the power of death, that is, the devil. In Psalm 116:3, we read about the Silent Suffering Messiah on the Cross as follows: The sorrows of death compassed me, and the pains of hell gat hold upon me: I found trouble and sorrow.

Therefore will I divide him a portion with the great, and he shall divide the spoil with the strong; because he hath poured out his soul unto death: and he was numbered with the transgressors; and he bare the sin of many, and made intercession for the transgressors. Isaiah 53:12

He will swallow up death in victory; and the Lord GOD will wipe away tears from off all faces; and the rebuke of his people shall he take away from off all the earth: for the LORD hath spoken it. Isaiah 25:8

The rejection of the Sinless, Dying Christ on the Cross by the Father may well have been the worst suffering the Messiah had to endure. This was the bitter cup of the Will of The Father that He was reluctant to drink. The breach in the eternal fellowship with the Father was the final isolation and abandonment that Jesus tasted. This is nothing less than the very essence of existence in Hell that would have been the destiny of Adam and all his seed, without any exception, if Christ would not go all the way.

And he made his grave with the wicked, and with the rich in his death; because he had done no violence, neither was any deceit in his mouth. Isaiah 53:9 Jesus was given the grave of Joseph of Arimathea- a devout rich man who had faith and hope in the Son of God. It is written that he begged Pontius Pilate that the body of Jesus may be given to him for burial.

Now, Jesus Christ is our High Priest in the New Covenant after the Order of Melchisedec, the Eternal Son, who lives forever, unlike the priests of the Old Covenant that the writer of Hebrews 7:23 says: … were not suffered to continue by reason of death.".

Again, in Hebrews 9:15 and 16 we read: "And for this cause He is the mediator of the new testament, that by means of death, for the redemption of the transgressions that were under the first testament, they which are called might receive the promise of eternal inheritance. For where a testament is, there must also of necessity be the death of the testator.".

Purpose of Christ's Death

The death of Jesus Christ led to all the seed of Adam being reconciled to God while we were still enemies of God. Thus, we read in Romans 5:10 For if, when we were enemies, we were reconciled to God by the death of his Son, much more, being reconciled, we shall be saved by his life. And again in Colossians 1:22, we see that Christ not only reconciled us in the body of his flesh through death, but also presented us holy and unblameable and unreproveable.

Jesus suffered the pains of death as we read in Peter's Spirit-filled sermon on the Day of Pentecost in Jerusalem, he said: Whom God hath raised up, having loosed the pains of death: because it was not possible that he should be holden of it. Acts 2:24. Christ being raised from the dead dies no more, we read in Romans 6:9, death does not have any dominion on Him anymore.

Partaking in the Death of Christ

In Romans 6:3-5, we read that those who are immersed into Jesus Christ were immersed into his death, so that as Christ was raised from the dead, we should walk in newness of life. As we have shared in the likeness of his death, we will be in the likeness of his resurrection.

The Church partaking of the bread and drinking the fruit of the vine in Holy Communion or at The Lord's Table signifies the death of Jesus, until He comes again. See 1 Corinthians 11:26 For as often as ye eat this bread, and drink this cup, ye do shew the Lord's death till he come.

Those who know Christ intimately desire to share in His death and sufferings, as Paul reveals in his letter to the Philippians 3:10 "That I may know him, and the power of his resurrection, and the fellowship of his sufferings, being made conformable unto his death". Again, Paul writes in 2 Corinthians 1:9 But we had the sentence of death in ourselves, that we should not trust in ourselves, but in God which raiseth the dead.

In 1 Corinthians 4:9, Paul writes: "For I think that God hath set forth us the apostles last, as it were appointed to death: for we are made a spectacle unto the world, and to angels, and to men." Apostles are, unlike modern day showbiz evangelism, appointed to death. In the second epistle to the Corinthians 4:11 and 12, Paul says: For we which live are alway delivered unto death for Jesus' sake, that the life also of Jesus might be made manifest in our mortal flesh. So then death worketh in us, but life in you.

The death of Christ caused judgment to be passed on Death. At the resurrection of the dead and living perfected Christians at the Rapture, the last enemy is destroyed. See 1 Corinthians 15:26 The last enemy that shall be destroyed is death.

Paradise inside the Earth until Jesus' Ascension
Following the death of the body of Jesus on the Cross, His Spirit went up to the Father and His Soul descended to the section of Hades where the souls of the righteous dead were being held captive and preached the gospel to them (I Peter 3.19). Those who believed in Him as the Promise given to Adam and Eve, He then carried to Paradise, in the heavenly realm, (Ephesians 4.8) in His victorious processional train.

When Jesus was crucified, there were two criminals hanging on crosses beside Him. One of them confessed his sin and repented and said to Jesus: (Luke 23:42,43) "Lord, remember me when you come into your kingdom. And Jesus said to him, Surely I say to you, Today shall you be with me in Paradise!"

Now we know from other Scriptures that Jesus did not go UP to his Father--God the Father of spirits--until after His resurrection! This is obvious from the story where Mary Magdalene stood outside the tomb weeping, because the body of her Lord had disappeared and she had seen Angels who told her that Jesus was alive, but because she didn't see Him anywhere, she was quite confused and broken up about it.

In this state, Jesus came to her in His resurrected body and said to her: "Woman why are you weeping!" She thinking him to be the gardener, said to him, "Sir, if you took away His body, please show me where you laid him, and I will take him away!" She didn't recognize Him! Then Jesus said, "Mary!" She suddenly recognized His voice and cried: "Rabboni" (Master). He said something very significant to her: In the tomb, He had not yet ASCENDED- GONE UP.. to see the Father! So that raises the question: If Jesus did not go up… where was He during this time, these three days? John 20:17

So, according to this and other Scriptures, in all the three days that His body was dead in the tomb, His spirit had not yet ASCENDED--GONE UP--to see the Father! So that raises the question: If Jesus' Spirit didn't go up… where was He during this time, these three days?

According to what He said to the thief, on the first day he was going to be in PARADISE with the thief! Now, if he had not gone UP to go see His Father in Paradise in

Heaven, He must have gone to another Paradise, where the Father obviously didn't live!

So there must have been at least TWO Heavenly Realms, at that time!

Chapter Eight
Sheol: Hades: Hell

"Never say, Go to Hell
For Hell is Real".
-Maafa-

SHEOL

The word 'Sheol' occurs sixty-five times in the Tanakh or the Hebrew Bible or the Old Testament. It is used most frequently in the Psalms, wisdom literature and prophetic books. This word sheol is derived from a root-word meaning "to ask," "demand;" hence insatiableness Proverbs 30: 15,16.

In Hebrew, Sheol (Sh'ol) is the "abode of the dead", the "Underworld", "the common grave of humankind" or "pit". It is a place where both the bad and the good, slave and king, pious and wicked must go at the point of death. Sheol is the destination of both the righteous and the unrighteous dead, as recounted in Ecclesiastes and Job. Hence, it is believed that there were two compartments in Sheol.

Sheol is sometimes compared to Hades. The word "hades" was in fact substituted for "sheol" when the Hebrew scriptures were translated into Greek (called the Septuagint). The New Testament (written in Greek) also uses "hades" to refer to the abode of the dead.

By the second century BC, Jews who accepted the Oral Torah had come to believe that those in sheol awaited the resurrection either in comfort (in theBosom of Abraham) or in torment. This belief is reflected in Jesus' narration of the destiny of Lazarus and the Rich Man. At that time Jews who rejected the Oral Torah believed that Sheol meant simply the grave.

Anglicans, who do not share a concept of "hades" with the Eastern Orthodox, have traditionally translated "sheol" (and "hades") as "hell" (for example in the King James Version). However, to avoid confusion of what are separate concepts in the Bible, modern English versions of the Bible tend either to transliterate the word sheol or use an alternative term such as the "grave" (e.g. the NIV). Roman Catholics generally translate "sheol" as "death."

The inhabitants of Sheol are "the congregation of the dead" Proverbs 21:16. As the term refers to the abode of the wicked Numbers 16:33 Job 24:19 Psalms 9:17 31:17 ; as well as the good Psalms 16:10 30:3 49:15 86:13, Sheol is described as being deep Job 11:8, dark Job 10:21, 22, with bars Job 17:16 and the dead are said to "go down" to it Numbers 16: 30,33 Ezekiel 31:15,16,17.

Sheol has Insatiable Desire

The corrupt desires (eyes and hearts) of sinners that desire the riches and pleasures of this world and finds so little satisfaction even in the gratification of them is like Sheol or hell and are equally insatiable, as we read in Proverbs 27:20 and Habbakuk 2:5.

Jonah and Jesus Raised from Sheol

First, it may not have been a whale, the word is a great fish which means it was one of considerable size. Also we find that God appointed this fish to swallow Jonah, as he appointed many other things of his creation that are recorded in the book of Jonah.

Many people believe that Jonah stayed alive in the fish for three days and that is the miracle but this is not what the Scripture portrays of this event. It says he cried from "Out of the belly of Sheol" not just the fish's belly. The Hebrew word for belly of Sheol is different than the belly of the fish, indicating two different areas.

The waters surrounded him even to his soul. This is an expression implying death (Ps.69:1. Jer.4:10) the deep closed, weeds wrapped around my head. His body sank to the moorings of the Mountains, where they begin (under land level). Showing he sank to the bottom before he was swallowed by the fish- which implies He died. While his soul went to the place of the dead, the fish comes and swallows up his body and it is preserved for 3 days.

The Bible says "The earth with its bars closed behind me forever." This is Old Testament language for sheol, the place of the dead. Job.38:17: "Have the gates of death been revealed to you? Or have you seen the doors of the shadow of death?

Isaiah 38:10 I said, "In the prime of my life I shall go to the gates of Sheol; I am deprived of the remainder of my years." Psalm 9:13 also mentions the gates of death. Sheol is the place of departed spirits the only way to get there is to die. Jonah is crying from the righteous portion of Sheol which is Abraham's bosom, (paradise) His soul went to Sheol while his body was swallowed in the fish preserved in its belly (abdomen). He recalls his last thoughts, When My soul fainted within me, that is a description of losing consciousness. He prayed before he died, then his body was scooped up and preserved in the whale for 3 days and nights.

This is why Jesus stated : For as Jonah was three days and three nights in the belly of the great fish, so will the Son of Man be three days and three nights in the heart of the earth. The men of Nineveh will rise up in the judgment with this generation and condemn it, because they repented at the preaching of Jonah; and indeed a greater than Jonah is here." (Matthew 12:40-41).

Luke 11:29-30:"This is an evil generation. It seeks a sign, and no sign will be given to it except the sign of Jonah the prophet. For as Jonah became a sign to the Ninevites, so also the Son of Man will be to this generation."

The sign Jesus is speaking of is his last to the unbelievers- His resurrection. The point Jesus is making is that Jonah was dead not alive for three days in the fish. If Jonah did not die then neither did Jesus because he is using him as a example of a miracle for his resurrection.

David Shown Mercy

David speaking of the forgiveness of God says in Psalm 86:13 that God delivered his soul from the depths of punishment in Hell: For great is thy mercy toward me: and thou hast delivered my soul from the lowest hell. God granted him repentance for the sins of murder and adultery.

HADES

The word "Hades" is transliterated (spelled by the sounds in the original language) from a Greek term that means the grave. The term "Hades" appears in the text of the New Testament as a translation of the Old Testament Sheol.

Like other first-century Jews literate in Greek, early Christians used the Greek word Hades to translate the Hebrew word Sheol. Thus, in Acts 2:27, the Hebrew phrase in Psalm 16:10 appears in the form: "you will not abandon my soul to Hades." Death and Hades are repeatedly associated in the Book of Revelation.

The word "Hades" appears in Jesus' promise to Peter: "And I also say unto thee, that thou art Peter, and upon this rock I will build my church; and the gates of Hades shall not prevail against it", and in the warning to Capernaum: "And thou, Capernaum, shalt thou be exalted unto heaven? thou shalt go down unto Hades." The word also appears in Luke's story of Lazarus and the rich man, which shows that Sheol/Hades, which had originally been seen as dark and gloomy, with little if any relation to afterlife rewards or punishments, had come to be understood as a place of comfort for the righteous ("in the bosom of Abraham ") and of torment for the wicked ("in anguish in this flame").

The Greek word "Hades" was translated into Latin as infernus (underworld) and passed into English as "hell," as in the King James Version of the above-cited New Testament passages. The word continued to be used to refer generically to the abode or situation of the dead, whether just or unjust, as in the Apostles' Creed, where it is said of Christ, "he descended into hell". But, except in

Greek, this generic usage of the word "Hades", "infernus", "hell" has become archaic and unusual. In Greek, the word (literally, "punishment," cf. Mathew 25:46, which speaks of "everlasting kolasis") is used to refer to what nowadays is usually meant by "hell" in English.

Hades has often been pictured as a place within the earth, rather than just a state of the soul.

The ancient Christian Churches hold that a final universal judgment will be pronounced on all human beings when soul and body are reunited in the resurrection of the dead. They also believe that, even while awaiting resurrection, the state of souls differs: "The souls of the righteous are in light and rest, with a foretaste of eternal happiness; but the souls of the wicked are in a state the reverse of this."

In Protestantism, it is believed that a person's destination is definitively sealed at death, and that the dead can neither assist the living nor be assisted by them. Some other sects, such as the Seventh Day Adventists, Jehovah's Witnesses, hold that, until the resurrection, the dead simply cease to exist or, if they exist at all, do so in a state of unconsciousness.

The Church Will overcome the Hordes of Hades
Matthew 16:18 8 {AND I ALSO} {TO THEE} {SAY,} {THAT} {THOU} {ART} {PETER,} {AND} {ON}

{THIS} {ROCK} {I WILL BUILD} {MY} {ASSEMBLY,} {AND} {GATES} {OF HADES} {SHALL NOT PREVAIL AGAINST} {IT.}

The Church of Jesus Christ built on the foundation of the Apostles and Prophets and their teachings with Jesus Himself as the Chief Cornerstone, will be severely attacked by the hordes of Hades- the very gates or might of Hades, but they will not be able to overcome the Church.

Proud Cities will be Thrust Down to Hades
Luke 10:15{AND} {THOU,} {CAPERNAUM,} {WHO} {TO} {THE} {HEAVEN} {HAST BEEN LIFTED UP,} <2193> {TO} {HADES} {THOU SHALT BE BROUGHT DOWN.}

Matthew 11:23   3   {AND}   {THOU,} {CAPERNAUM,} {WHO} {TO}   {THE} {HEAVEN} {HAST BEEN LIFTED UP,} {TO} {HADES} {SHALT BE BROUGHT DOWN:} {FOR} {IF} {IN} {SODOM} {HAD TAKEN PLACE} {THE} {WORKS OF POWER} {WHICH} {HAVE TAKEN PLACE} {IN} {THEE,} {IT HAD REMAINED} {UNTIL} {TODAY.} The cities of the world that boasted great deeds, splendour and pomp but never honoured God will be brought down to Hades.

The Rich Man went down to Hades
Luke 16:23 {AND} {IN}   {THE}   {HADES}
{HAVING LIFTED UP} {HIS EYES,} {BEING} {IN}
{TORMENTS,} {HE SEES} {ABRAHAM} {AFAR OFF,}
{AND} {LAZARUS} {IN} {HIS BOSOM.}

After the Bodily Death of Jesus on the Cross
Acts 2:27 {FOR} {NOT} {THOU WILT LEAVE} {SOUL}
{MY} {IN} {HADES}   {NOR} {WILT THOU GIVE}
{HOLY ONE} {THY} {TO SEE} {CORRUPTION.}

   Acts   2:31   {FORESEEING}   {HE   SPOKE}
{CONCERNING} {THE} {RESURRECTION} {OF
THE} {CHRIST,} {THAT} {WAS NOT LEFT} {SOUL}
{HIS} {IN} {HADES} {NOR}   {FLESH} {HIS} {SAW}
{CORRUPTION.}

   The words cited above declare that Jesus' body when it
lay in the tomb did not suffer corruption. The Holy Spirit
brooded over the body of Jesus while His Soul went down
to Hades to preach to the righteous dead and take them
with Him to Paradise. He who knew no sin was made SIN
for the whole world. He is the Lamb that was slain before
the Foundation of the world in the Eternal Counsel of
God. The Holy Spirit brought the Sacrifice to the Father.
The powers of decay and corruption could not work in the
sinless flesh of the Holy One of Israel.

Hades emptied of Righteous Dead by Jesus
1 Cor 15:55 {WHERE} {OF THEE,} {O DEATH,}
{THE} {STING?} {WHERE} {OF THEE,} {O HADES}
{THE} {VICTORY?}

Revelation 1:18 {AND} {THE} {LIVING [ONE]:}
{AND} {I BECAME} {DEAD,} {AND} {BEHOLD}
{ALIVE} {I AM} {TO} {THE} {AGES} {OF THE}
{AGES,} {AMEN} {AND} {HAVE} {THE} {KEYS} {OF}
{HADES} {AND} {OF DEATH.}

The sting of death was made powerless- both physical
and eternal death and the power of Hades to receive all
the dead were nullified. Jesus has the Keys of Hades and
Death today. The wicked and the righteous, all who died
until now, (except for the Man Christ Jesus), have not yet
got their resurrection body.

Angel of Death and Hades
Revelation 6:8 {AND} {I SAW,} {AND} {BEHOLD,} {A
HORSE} {PALE,} {AND} {HE} {SITTING} {ON} {IT,}
{NAME} {HIS [WAS]} {DEATH,} {AND} {HADES}
{FOLLOWS} {WITH} {HIM;} {AND} {WAS GIVEN}
{TO THEM} {AUTHORITY} {TO KILL} {OVER}
{THE} {FOURTH} {OF THE} {EARTH} {WITH}
{SWORD} {AND} {WITH} {FAMINE} {AND} {WITH}
{DEATH,} {AND} {BY} {THE} {BEASTS} {OF THE}
{EARTH.}

The Sea, Death and Hades give up the Dead
Revelation 20:13 {AND} {GAVE UP} {THE} {SEA} {THE} {IN} {IT} {DEAD,} {AND} {DEATH} {AND} {HADES} {GAVE UP} {THE} {IN} {THEM} {DEAD;} {AND} {THEY WERE JUDGED} {EACH} {ACCORDING TO} {THEIR WORKS:}

The souls of the unrighteous dead are released from the sea, Death and Hades to be judged according to their works before the White Throne of God. The souls of the righteous dead, it may be remembered have already been taken up to Heaven.

Death and Hades Cast into Lake of Fire
Revelation 20:14 {AND} {DEATH} {AND} {HADES} {WERE CAST} {INTO} {THE} {LAKE} {OF FIRE.} {THIS} {IS} {THE} {SECOND} {DEATH.}

The contents of Death and Hades- viz., souls of the unrighteous dead were cast into the lake of fire which is the second death, from which there is no return.

Destruction or Abaddon
The King or the Angel of the bottomless pit is called Abaddon or Destruction, the Hebrew name (equivalent to the Greek Apollyon, i.e., destroyer) "Revelation 9:11 It is rendered "destruction" in Job 28:22; 31:12; 26:6; Proverbs 15:11 27:20. In the last three of these passages the Revised Version retains the word "Abaddon."

The Grave

The grave is referred to as qeber in Hebrew and mnemion in Greek. It is the place where the dead body is placed and not to be confused with Sheol or Hades where consciousness is described.

The body taken from the dust returns to the dust. God does not keep in memory the particles making up the original body. The original body never rises from death; it returns to dust (Job 14:12). God gives each person a new body in the resurrection (I Cor. 15:35-54; 2. Cor. 5: 1-8; Phil. 3:21).

The soul and spirit, called the inner man, are immortal and continue in full consciousness between death and resurrection of the body, and in the new resurrected body into all eternity. The process of separation of the spirit and soul from the body in biological/physical death will continue until sin is put down and death is destroyed (Rev. 21:3-7; 22:3).

Soul-Sleep Not taught in Scripture

Let us examine the texts that are used by the false cults that advocate soul-sleep:

1. Sleep in the dust (Job 7:21; Ps 22:15; 146:4; Eccl. 3:19-20; Dan. 12:2). Only the body that is made of dust will return to the dust. The soul and spirit are not made

of material substances as the body so they will not turn to dust.

2. Death- a falling asleep (Acts 7:60; 13:36; I Cor. 15:6, 18, 20, 51; I Thess. 4:13-17; 5:10; 2 Pet. 3:4). No one can see the invisible part of man- the soul and spirit whether it falls asleep. It is only the body that men can see as falling asleep. The body falls asleep when the spirit leaves it (James 2:26). In Acts 13:36, that which fell asleep was laid in a tomb and saw corruption. That seeing corruption refers to the flesh is clear from Psalm 16:10, Acts 2:23-32).

3. Death is spoken of as sleep (Deut. 31:16; 2. Sam. 7:12; I Kings 2.10; 11:21, 43). This also refers to the body falling asleep as in the above cases.

4. No difference between man and beast in death (Eccl. 3:19-20). The false cults use this text to say that both man and beast become extinct at death. As men and beast are made of dust only as far as the body is concerned. The same passage makes the distinction in saying that the spirit of man goes upward and the spirit of beast goes downward to the earth.

5. No consciousness in death (Psalm 6:5). Consciousness is not in the chemical makeup of the body for then it would continue even after the spirit leaves the body. When the spirit and soul leave the body, it is dead and hence the body cannot be conscious. Remembrance is

a function of the spirit and soul, not of the brain, though the brain may be used in the process in the earthly life. Giving of thanks is done in heaven, not in the grave or in hell.

6. The dead praise not the Lord (Psalm 115:17). The dead body cannot praise God. The souls of the righteous continue to praise God in full consciousness after leaving their bodies (Heb.12:22, 23; Rev. 6:9-11), but the wicked who go to hell will not praise God (Isaiah 14:9-11).

7. In the day of death his thoughts perish (Psalm 146:4). The body cannot have any thoughts when the inner man departs. After leaving the body, souls and spirits continue to have thoughts in heaven (Rev.6:9-11) and in hell (Isa.14:9-11; Luke 16.19-31).

8. The dead know not anything (Job 14:21; Ecc. 9:5-6). The body cannot know anymore after death, but the soul and spirit continue to know and have emotions and desires after leaving the body.

9. The dead come out of the graves (Matt.27:52; John 5:28-29). The soul and spirit never go to the graves.

10. David is not yet ascended into heaven (Acts 2:34). This is only true as to the body of David, but not as to his soul and spirit. All souls who died before the resurrection of Christ were taken to heaven as captives (Psa. 68:18; Eph. 4:8-10).

Every just man's spirit is in heaven (Heb.12:22-23).

One does not die spiritually at physical death, for one is either dead or alive spiritually in one's lifetime. If he is spiritually dead in sins, his soul will go to hell at physical death. If he is alive spiritually at physical death, his soul will go immediately to heaven and his body to the grave until their reunion in the first resurrection. Acts 13:36 reveals that as David's body saw corruption; it shows the part that has not yet ascended.

Thus soul sleep is fallacy, body sleep is reality.

The Pit

The soul of the unrighteous dead enters Hades through the pit. In Job 33:24, 30, the decline of a soul through sin into the spiritual region of the dead, or the eternal loss of one's soul is declared to be pre-empted by the ransom (paid by Jesus of His Own Blood). We are to profit from the power of life of the flesh in the blood before we are laid low in the grave (Psalms 30.9).

The horrible pit of Hades is referred to in Psalms 40:2 as a pit of noise. (He brought me up also out of an horrible pit, out of the miry clay, and set my feet upon a rock, and established my goings. {an…: Heb. a pit of noise}). In Psalms 88:6 we see the Pit as having deeps and being a place of darkness, in Psalms 55.23 of the pit of destruction and Psalms 57:6 of the pit of snares and net that the wicked lay for the righteous. In Psalms 69.15, we see that the Pit has a mouth that can close on the soul to swallow it.

As the dead body is laid in wholeness in the grave, the soul enters wholly into the pit (if it is not redeemed by God) as we read in Proverbs 1:12 Let us swallow them up alive as the grave; and whole, as those that go down into the pit.

The Pit will seek the soul of that man who does violence to the life of any person. The Deceiver of the nations is brought down to hell to the sides of the pit, to the very bottom of the pit. See Isaiah 14:15 Yet thou shalt be brought down to hell, to the sides of the pit.

God has loved our soul when we were spiritually in the pit or heading for eternal destruction. We see that in Isaiah 38:17…..but thou hast in love to my soul delivered it from the pit of corruption: for thou hast cast all my sins behind thy back. {Heb. thou hast loved my soul from the pit}

There is no worship of God in the grave or the pit as we read in Isaiah 38:18 For the grave cannot praise thee, death can not celebrate thee: they that go down into the pit cannot hope for thy truth.

The finality of bodily death as the termination of mortal existence is equated with the power of the grave as Job speaks in Job 7:9 As the cloud is consumed and vanisheth away: so he that goeth down to the grave shall come up no more.

Those righteous Jews in the Old Testament who humbled themselves and sought God were said to have died in peace and were said to be gathered to their fathers as in the case of King Josiah in II Chronicles 34:28.

Job writes of God's judgment as coming past death and the grave in Job 14:13 O that thou would hide me in the grave, that thou would keep me secret, until thy wrath be past, that thou would appoint me a set time, and remember me!

All the children of Adam, including Christians who do not partake in the Rapture (Secret Second Advent of Jesus Christ) will be laid low in the grave, though their sins are forgiven. See Job 24:19 Drought and heat consume the snow waters: so does the grave those, which have sinned. {consume: Heb. violently take}

The Psalmist considers his life as drawing closer to the grave when he is heavily afflicted. See Psalms 88:3 For my soul is full of troubles: and my life draws nigh unto the grave.

The mercy of God is to be declared in this earthly life. Those who are in hell cannot speak of the faithfulness of God. See Psalms 88:11 Shall thy lovingkindness be declared in the grave? or thy faithfulness in destruction?

See also Psalms 6:5 For in death there is no remembrance of thee: in the grave who shall give thee thanks?

The infinite capacity of the grave to swallow dead bodies is written in Proverbs 30:16 The grave; and the barren womb; the earth that is not filled with water; and the fire that says not, It is enough.

Scripture tells the people of the world to engage themselves usefully in this world as there is no wisdom or beneficial activity in death or beyond the grave for those who do not have hope in the world. See Ecclesiastes 9:10 Whatsoever thy hand findeth to do, do it with thy might; for there is no work, nor device, nor knowledge, nor wisdom, in the grave, whither thou goest.

The Love of God is considered as strong as death and the grave. Songs of Solomon 8:6 Set me as a seal upon thine heart, as a seal upon thine arm: for love is strong as death; jealousy is cruel as the grave: the coals thereof are coals of fire, which hath a most vehement flame. {cruel: Heb. hard}.

Tartarus

On one occasion the King James Bible erroneously renders the word tartarus, as hell. Tartarus means "abyss--a place of restraint," (also called "the deepest abyss of the Greek hades"). The word tartarus can be traced to the underworld of the pagan Egyptians. Tartarus is an Egyptian word, not

Greek. And this one-time use in the King James clearly has reference to angels being held in restraint until their (not our) judgment.

"For if God spared not the angels that sinned, but cast them down to hell [tartarus--abyss], and delivered them into chains of darkness, to be reserved unto judgment" (II Pet 2:4). And this place of restraint ("chains of darkness") is only until we (I Cor. 6:3) judge the angels' "judgment", not for eternity. The apocryphal book Enoch, chapter 20, verse 2 specifically states that Tartarus is the place in which the angels who cohabited with women in Genesis 6 are to be reserved for judgment.

The Bottomless Pit

In the spirit realm either in outer space or inside the earth, there is the bottomless pit that however can cause a smoke that darkens the sky. See Revelation 9:2 And he opened the bottomless pit; and there arose a smoke out of the pit, as the smoke of a great furnace; and the sun and the air were darkened by reason of the smoke of the pit.

The Beast that controls the world's commerce after Jesus has removed the Church from the earth is a spirit that ascends from the bottomless pit. See Revelation 11:7 And when they shall have finished their testimony, the beast that ascendeth out of the bottomless pit shall make war against them, and shall overcome them, and shall kill them.

Revelation 17:8 The beast that thou sawest was, and is

not; and shall ascend out of the bottomless pit, and go into perdition: and they that dwell on the earth shall wonder, whose names were not written in the book of life from the foundation of the world, when they behold the beast that was, and is not, and yet is.

Satan is bound and cast into the bottomless pit for a thousand years so that the world may see the reign of righteousness of Christ and His saints. Revelation 20:1 And I saw an angel come down from heaven, having the key of the bottomless pit and a great chain in his hand.

Revelation 20:3 And cast him into the bottomless pit, and shut him up, and set a seal upon him, that he should deceive the nations no more, till the thousand years should be fulfilled: and after that he must be loosed a little season.

Those who go down into the bottomless pit cannot praise God, nor hope in the truth of God, if they had believed in the Father of lies all their life. Isaiah 38:18

The ultimate triumph of Jesus over death and the power of the grave to swallow dead bodies is marked in the victory shout of the Christians who will rise from the earth when Jesus returns to catch them away to Heaven.

O death, where is thy sting?
O grave, where is thy victory?
1 Corinthians 15:55

Chapter Nine
The Rich man and Lazarus (the Beggar)
Luke 16:19-31

19 There was a certain rich man, which was clothed in purple and fine linen, and fared sumptuously every day:

20 And there was a certain beggar named Lazarus, which was laid at his gate, full of sores,

21 And desiring to be fed with the crumbs that fell from the rich man's table: moreover the dogs came and licked his sores.

22 And it came to pass, that the beggar died, and was carried by the angels into Abraham's bosom: the rich man also died, and was buried;

23 And in hell (Hades) he lift up his eyes, being in torments, and seeth Abraham afar off, and Lazarus in his bosom.

24 And he cried and said, Father Abraham, have mercy on me, and send Lazarus, that he may dip the tip of his finger in water, and cool my tongue; for I am tormented in this flame.

25 But Abraham said, Son, remember that thou in thy lifetime received thy good things, and likewise Lazarus evil things: but now he is comforted, and thou art tormented.

26 And beside all this, between us and you there is a great gulf fixed: so that they which would pass from hence to you cannot; neither can they pass to us that would come from thence.

27 Then he said, I pray thee therefore, father, that thou wouldest send him to my father's house:

28 For I have five brethren; that he may testify unto them, lest they also come into this place of torment.

29 Abraham saith unto him, They have Moses and the prophets; let them hear them.

30 And he said, Nay, father Abraham: but if one went unto them from the dead, they will repent.

31 And he said unto him, If they hear not Moses and the prophets, neither will they be persuaded, though one rose from the dead.

The conscious soul

It may be seen from the verse below that Rachel's soul left her body at death even as she was being delivered of her baby- Benjamin (Benoni). Gen. 35:18 And it came to pass, as her (Rachel's) soul was in departing, (for she died) that she called his name Benoni."

The soul seems to have a kind of body (with eyes, tongue etc.,) with clear memory and reasoning, perceiving heat, cold, touch, bliss and torment already before the final judgment of the soul and before it is accorded an everlasting body.

Many otherwise intelligent and educated people of this world are wholly convinced that the thought realm is entirely to do with the head or the brain. They are in for a surprise, the moment after the physical eyes close in death in this world and the eyes of the soul open in eternity. The Bible tells us clearly what to expect beyond the grave. Numerous Near Death (NDEs) and After Death experiences (ADEs) corroborate the Bible account.

The 'soul body' continues to exist without food, drink or nourishment. However, the rich man vividly feels the acute heat, pain, torment and thirst. Memory and remorse in connection with the earthly life are well preserved, showing that despite the death of the physical, earthly body and brain, these faculties are not lost. Dives, the Rich Man, is able to see Lazarus being comforted at the bosom of Abraham. We should note that Dives does not question the fairness in the explanation of their respective destinies.

The Old Testament indicates that the appearance of the soul after decease is clearly recognisable as similar to the earthly/bodily appearance and even conversation between a deceased soul and the living is possible, though not encouraged by God. The conversation between Samuel and the fallen king Saul in I Samuel 28: 7-20 is illustrative of total consciousness of a departed soul and comprehensive communication between two persons- one in the realm of the dead and the other still in the earthly existence.

The souls of Moses and Elijah appeared on the Mount of Transfiguration conversing with Jesus and they were even recognized by Peter though they had never seen Moses and Elijah in their lives. Mark 9:5 And Peter answered and said to Jesus, Master, it is good for us to be here: and let us make three tabernacles; one for thee, and one for Moses, and one for Elijah.

Sadducees, Pharisees & The Resurrection

The Sadducees were in political power and were the aristocratic class. The Pharisees were followers of mammon. Both these groups were wealthy. They had a wrong sense of value and had denied the reality of their own situation. Jesus appealed to their hearts as the chosen people had drifted far from the purity of doctrine that God had given, picking up ideas from pagan religions. While the Sadducees did not believe in the resurrection, the Pharisees, were a sect of the Jews who believed in the resurrection and afterlife in theory, and hence Jesus was challenging their rejection of what "Moses and the prophets" taught about death.

Poverty glorified

The early Christians glorified poverty and shared their wealth and income, in full understanding of the poverty of Jesus that had made so many truly rich. This is exactly the opposite of what the Pharisees expected would happen to a man like Lazarus. It was assumed that such people were poor and diseased beggars because they were under God's curse. Therefore, they thought that it was only natural that such people go to be tormented in Hades when they die.

The rebuke is directed at the selfishness of the Jewish leaders and wealthy people who justified their imagined status with God by the theory that they were blessed because of their piety (John 9:2,3).

COVETOUSNESS-
FROM THE LEAST TO THE GREATEST
"You cannot serve God and mammon."
Jesus' Sermon on the Mount

Someone once asked an evangelist what hell was like. The man of God said, "Hell is selfishness on fire!" This is the primary warning from Jesus in the account of Lazarus and Dives. The vanity of expensive garments (purple and fine linen) and the daily gluttony (faring sumptuously) of the wealthy are attacked fair and square. Many of the Pharisees and Saducees were members of the great Sanhedrin, rulers of synagogues, who by various methods, amassed to themselves great riches, and even devoured widows' houses. Abraham tells Dives the way things stand. "All your life you loved riches and had no time for the likes of Lazarus. But I do have time for the likes of Lazarus, and now he is with me, and you have nothing."

"And the Pharisees also, who were covetous (money lovers), heard all these things: and they derided him. And he said unto them, Ye are they which justify yourselves before men; but God knoweth your hearts: for that which is highly esteemed among men is abomination in the sight of God. Luke 6.15

Covetousness is the evil that permeates all sections of society from the poorest to the richest. It is marked by the unceasing desire to possess things, money and wealth. The poor initially desire to have their basic needs met, but after they are met, they find their needs mushrooming into wants, in exactly the same way as the rich.

"What do you suggest for a woman who has everything, and isn't happy with any of it?"

This is what God records in Jeremiah 8:10 ….. for every one from the least even unto the greatest is given to covetousness, from the prophet even unto the priest every one deals falsely. We have a responsibility to those less fortunate than ourselves. God measures spiritual greatness differently than we tend to. Many of the most miserable on this earth will have the most splendid homes in heaven.

The Infinitely and Truly Wealthy Son of God from

Heaven possessing lasting riches, the Lord Jesus Christ, became an incredibly small being, the Poorest Person on planet earth. He was stripped of all glory and majesty and put to death in the body as though he were a common criminal, to carry all our sin and shame. He is the One who encouraged us to store up treasure in Heaven and gave us the account of Dives to warn all those who desire to be rich in this world.

Paul the Apostle, warns the wealthy believers and those who aspire to riches in 1 Timothy 6:9 But they that will be rich fall into temptation and a snare, and into many foolish and hurtful lusts, which drown men in destruction and perdition.

Tongue- An unruly evil

A literal drop of water on the rich man's tongue would hardly solve his problem of burning in the torment of hell, but his agony and torment was so intense that even a 'moment' of relief would have been tremendous. This is again speaking of the translation in eternity of the total lack of mercy that the extremely wealthy have towards the poorest on the planet.

It also speaks of the misuse of the tongue in blaspheming the God of heaven and slandering and gossiping about fellow men. Every sinner has sinned more in speech than in deed. The wealth of the rich makes him presumptuous in thinking that he can talk arrogantly. The Psalmist says that the tongue of the rich man goes through the whole earth (Psalm 73).

The Great Gulf

The gulf between Dives and Lazarus that was entirely due to the lack of sensitivity in the heart of the rich man in the world has been translated in eternity into a transparent gulf that permits sight and communication, but not travel across for people on either side of it. The painfulness of the torment in hell is made even worse for Dives when he is able to see Lazarus in Abraham's bosom being comforted.

On earth, Lazarus was at the gate of Dives and was considered an eye sore to him. There was no way, Lazarus could even dream of partaking of the table of the rich man. He only desired to eat of the crumbs that fell from the table, but the dogs were feeding on the sores of his public misery.

Walls of the Wealthy

The European Union by its Schengen wall, effectively and militantly, protects its material wealth from the poor in the nations surrounding it. The nationals permitted to visit the European Union are essentially Europeans from North America and Australia & New Zealand, and the wealthiest of other nations.

The eternal truth is that every man, woman and child is created in the image of God and the terms European, African, Asian etc., are all inventions to divide the children of Adam.

The gulf in eternity is also the translation of the gulf in people's hearts of unforgiveness and resentment that prevent them from loving and accepting their fellow men, as God for Christ's sake has loved and forgiven us.

There was also a gulf between eternity and the physical world on earth. But for the extremely few exceptions of those who were raised or revived from the dead, the overwhelming majority never return to the mortal life again.

The rich man could remember his brothers and wanted Lazarus to go back to the world and warn them about what was awaiting them, if they did not repent. John Bunyan, writing in his book- Visions of Heaven and Hell, about what his soul saw in the visitation of heaven and hell, reports that the people in hell are devoid of any empathy and those who practised and provoked each other to sinful pleasures on earth, were tormenting each other so much the more in hell. Hence, he says that Dives was not showing true concern for his brothers, but only keen that they do not come there to torment him.

The Danger of Unbelief

Jesus wanted the Pharisees to see their danger in persistent unbelief. The beggar's name is significant. Jesus had raised Lazarus of Bethany but the Pharisees, to whom the story was primarily addressed, still refused to recognize Jesus as the life giver, even though they claimed to believe in the resurrection. They would be at serious risk of rejecting Him even after His own phenomenal resurrection (John 12:42).

Jesus- Son of Abraham

Jesus pointed out the misguided reverence of the Jews for Abraham. The rich man, instead of calling on God, actually prays to Abraham for mercy as if the patriarch were in charge of his destiny. He calls him "Father Abraham" when only our Father in heaven is our spiritual father (Matt. 23:9; 6:9). The Jews imagined their spiritual and political status to depend on their lineage as sons of Abraham (Luke 3:8).

The Jews challenged Jesus (John 8:53) Art thou greater than our father Abraham, which is dead? and the prophets are dead: whom makest thou thyself? To the believing Martha, Jesus said: I am the resurrection, and the life: he that believeth in me, though he were dead, yet shall he live (John 11.25).

In Matthew 3:9, John the Baptist told the Jews: "…

think not to say within yourselves, We have Abraham to our father: for I say unto you, that God is able of these stones to raise up children unto Abraham". God is One who creates life and can even impart life to lifeless stones or spiritually dead people.

> Jesus on His triumphal entry to Jerusalem, when "…the whole multitude of the disciples began to rejoice and praise God with a loud voice, and some of the Pharisees from among the multitude asked Him to rebuke the disciples, Jesus said: I tell you that, if these should hold their peace, the stones would immediately cry out. (Luke 19:37-40).

God is the One who imparts His praises to His people and can cause even stones to break forth with praise and the trees of the field to clap their hands (Isaiah 55.12).

Job and Abraham were very wealthy men, but they were far wealthier in their faith in God. Their hearts were not filled with earthly goals. Abraham looked for a city which hath foundations, whose builder and maker is God." (Hebrews 11:8-10). Abraham's faith objective was the heavenly city. Ungodly wealthy men of the world do not abhor evil as Job did. Job and Abraham are types of Christ. But Jesus came and died as a poor man.

Bosom of Abraham or Paradise

Jesus told the penitent thief on the cross: "Today you will be with me in paradise" (Luke 23:43). This makes Paradise the place where both Jesus and the repentant thief went after their deaths; this is the paradise of the righteous, also called the "Bosom of Abraham" (Luke 16:22). Paradise was the abode of the souls of the just and identified with part of Hades or hell. Here the souls of the just were in blissful rest and awaited the Messiah to lead them to heaven.

The gates of heaven were not opened until Jesus ascended to the Father. When Jesus ascended to heaven, Scripture tells us that He "led a host of captives" (Eph. 4:8). Now, who were these captives and where were they being held captive? They were the righteous souls of the just men and women who were awaiting heaven's gate to open. Keep in mind that heaven had been closed as a result of the sin of Adam and Eve.

The Spirit of the Law is established by Jesus

In the only narration of Jesus that was not a parable, He established the Law and showed that it was not enough to be a child of Abraham after the flesh. Note that Abraham calls Dives- 'Son' and Dives calls Abraham, 'Father'! Both were probably born Jews. The tragedy of the rich man was that he did not believe that the Law and the Prophets was God's very Word and just as reliable as the report of one returning from the dead. Let us take careful note of the last words in the narration of the most gripping true story ever told: Those who do not take the Law seriously, will not take the testimony of Jesus and His resurrection seriously either.

Jesus established the Law indeed and showed that the twofold nature of the Law in loving God and the fellow man will always be valid as the fount of the One True Faith. In other words, those who love God will love their neighbour and in doing so, will receive greater and greater light, peace, joy and love in knowing the Son of God- Jesus Christ of Nazareth, the Author and Giver of Eternal life.

The Blessed Jesus has, by eternal virtue of His Holy Sacrifice, removed the need for animal sacrifices and the rituals of washings and many, though not all, of the ordinances of the Old Testament.

Chapter Ten
Second Death
The Terror of The Lord
(The Lake Of Fire)

And death and hell were cast into the lake of fire.
This is the second death.
Revelation 20:14

The word, "hell," is translated from the Hebrew, sheol, or
the Greek, hades, which refer to the unseen world, or the

world of the dead. Another Greek word, also translated as "hell" has a quite different meaning and tends to confuse many. When Jesus spoke of everlasting punishment, he did not use the words Hades, or Sheol, he used the term Gehenna. The Greek, Ge-enna means a place of burning. In most Bibles, this word is simply translated as "Hell," even though early Christian writers usually used the term Gehenna, the fiery pit, to mean hell. In addition, this dark place matches the term's traditional meaning, a dark pit in which the Supreme God has cast his spirit enemies.

The Second Death is actually an everlasting soul in an everlasting body, suffering unending torment due to the undying worms of conscience and the bodily tortures of Satan and his demons in liquid fire and sulphur. The first and most tragic aspect of the second death is that, while the judgment passed on Adam was revoked and made reversible, due to the atonement by Christ, the second death is IRREVERSIBLE.

There are many who believe that hell is only for a limited duration or terminating in annihilation. The doctrine of universal salvation that some Christians believe in implies that the fires of Gehenna are purgatorial and that after a long age, all souls will be saved. But examination of the Greek equivalent "aion" and "aionios" of the English words- "eternity and everlasting" show that the same terms are used as for the everlasting nature of God and heaven as for everlasting punishment.

Matthew 25:46
And these shall go away into everlasting punishment but the righteous into life eternal. (KJV)

And these shall go away to punishment age-during, but the righteous to life age-during.' (Young's Literal Translation).

The Lord decrees that those who take part in the First Resurrection are holy and the second death shall have no power on them (Revelation 20:6 Blessed and holy is he that hath part in the first resurrection: on such the second death hath no power, but they shall be priests of God and of Christ, and shall reign with him a thousand years.)

Sinners and Wicked on their Way to Hell
The majority of the world's people are on the broad way to destruction. Those who are on the narrow way to eternal life are few. Read Matthew 7:13. In Proverbs 11:19, we see that righteousness tends to life, but those who pursue evil pursue it to their own death.

Because most people are choosing their own way to destruction, God found it necessary to repeat the following words in Proverbs 14:12 and Proverbs 16:25: "There is a way which seems right unto a man, but the end thereof are the ways of death."

THE MANY: It is the many that open their eternity in Hellfire. The Psalmist sees the end of the wicked in Psalm 55:15 Let death seize upon them, and let them go down quick into hell: for wickedness is in their dwellings, and among them.

MANY THERE BE (that perish)-Matthews 7:13

MANY...many...many-Matthew 7:22 (three groups of many)

MANY ARE CALLED (but they perish)-Matthew 22:14

MANY...SEEK TO ENTER IN (to heaven), AND SHALL NOT BE ABLE-Luke 13:24

Many deceived-Matthew 24:5

Many deceived-Matthew 24:11

MANY...ARE THE ENEMIES OF THE CROSS OF CHRIST-Philippians 3:18

MANY...WHOSE END IS DESTRUCTION-Philippians 3:18,19

MANY...DECEIVERS-Titus 1:10

MANY...CORRUPT THE WORD OF GOD- 2 Corinthians 2:17

THEY PROFESS THAT THEY KNOW GOD; BUT... (are) * REPROBATE-Titus 1:16

SATAN...DECEIVETH THE WHOLE WORLD-
Revelation 12:9

Fear of God

The righteous can say the words in Psalm 56:13 For thou hast delivered my soul from death: wilt not thou deliver my feet from falling, that I may walk before God in the light of the living?

Jesus warned us to fear God who can kill the body and then cast the soul in an everlasting body into everlasting hellfire. That was why the Christian martyrs went boldly to their deaths. Fearing God removes every form of guilt, fear and shame that is brought by sin or the fear of man. In Proverbs 14:27, we see that the fear of the Lord which is the beginning of wisdom, to be "a fountain of life, to depart from the snares of death.".

The Lord Jesus Christ is the One who died and has the keys of hell and death Revelation 1:18 I am he that lives, and was dead; and, behold, I am alive for evermore, Amen; and have the keys of hell and of death.

Consider the following two verses from the Gospels:
Matthew 10:28 {AND} {YE SHOULD NOT FEAR} {BECAUSE OF} {THOSE WHO} {KILL} {THE} {BODY,} {BUT THE} {SOUL} {ARE NOT ABLE} {TO KILL;} {BUT YE SHOULD FEAR} {RATHER} {HIM

WHO} {IS ABLE} {BOTH} {SOUL} {AND} {BODY}
{TO DESTROY} {IN} {GEHENNA.}

Luke 12:5{ BUT I WILL SHEW} {YOU} {WHOM}
{YE SHOULD FEAR:} {FEAR} {HIM WHO} {AFTER}
{BEING KILLED,} {AUTHORITY} {HAS} {TO CAST}
{INTO} {THE} {GEHENNA;} {YEA,} {I SAY} {TO
YOU,} {HIM} {FEAR.}

Defeated Christians in Danger of Hellfire

The Apostle of Love- John the Divine in 1 John 3:14 truly
points out that we know that we have passed from death
unto life, because we love the brethren. He that loveth not
his brother abideth in death.

When Jesus, through John- the apostle, told the
Church: ...... He that overcomes shall not be hurt of
the second death (Revelation 2:11), it is implied that the
believer who does not overcome the power of sin in the
flesh, the world and Satan may well be hurt by the second
death.

In Revelation 2:23, we read the Holy Jesus stating
these solemn words to the church in Thyatira: And I will
kill her children with death; and all the churches shall
know that I am he which searcheth the reins and hearts:
and I will give unto every one of you according to your
works.

In Revelation 12:11, we read of the Christians who

overcame Satan by the blood of the Lamb, and by the word of their testimony; and they loved not their lives unto the death.

Yakob (James) The Just, brother of Our Lord says in chapter 5 of his epistle, verse 20 that the Christian who converts the sinner (i.e., the backslider from the error of his way) shall save a soul from death and hide a multitude of sins.

Paul writing in Romans 6:16 says that we are servants to whom we yield ourselves to obey- whether of sin unto death, or obedience unto righteousness. The fruit of yielding to sin and death is something that makes us ashamed of thinking back of those deeds of disobedience to God or servility to sin. The end of those things is said to be death- death, then indeed not just of the body, but of the soul (Romans 6:21).

The wages of sin is death, before and after salvation (see Romans 6:23). When a Christian is in the flesh and walking after the flesh, the motions of sin in the members of the body bring forth fruit unto death (Romans 7:5). Hence, the keeping of the commandment which is meant for life, carried the power of death when disobeyed due to the weakness of the flesh. (Romans 7:10).

The commandment that carried death if disobeyed thus made sin exceeding sinful (Romans 7:13). Finally, the poor apostle discovers himself trapped in a body of death and cries out in his wretched misery (Romans 7:24). In 1 Corinthians 15:56 we read that the sting of death is sin; and the strength of sin is the law.

Smell of Life and Smell of Death

When a true Christian is met by a person who is not on the way of life, the smell of death and judgment is encountered by that person. When a true Christian is met by a person on the way of life or desiring to be delivered from his sinful ways, the aroma of life is encountered. Thus we read in II Corinthians 2:16 To the one we are the savour of death unto death; and to the other the savour of life unto life. And who is sufficient for these things?

Sorrow unto Life and Sorrow unto Death

Moreover while godly sorrow works repentance unto salvation, the sorrow of the world is a kind that is without hope of eternal life and hence works only death (2 Corinthians 7:10 For godly sorrow worketh repentance to salvation not to be repented of: but the sorrow of the world worketh death.).

Mortal Sins

There are sins that require the death of the body for the soul and the spirit to be redeemed. There are other sins that a Christian may commit that a brother can intercede for as the Apostle of Love points out in I John 5:16 If any man see his brother sin a sin which is not unto death, he shall ask, and he shall give him life for them that sin not unto death. There is a sin unto death: I do not say that he shall pray for it.

Mind- The Battleground between Life and Death

The body of flesh is made up of the elements and the sun's energy that is in the food that is consumed- hence, all of us are global citizens in our body. The murders of nationalistic wars have been more than the wars of religion. Religion has only provided a pretext for killing to own more lands, houses, gold, slaves and cattle.

The war between the soul of man and the powers of darkness are being fought over the battlefield of the mind where thoughts, images and imaginations are sown by the Wicked One or by God as both are given the possibility for the same.

The thoughts of pride, hatred, bitterness, strife and uncleanness are the seeds of death in all three- spirit, soul and body. The thoughts of a spiritual mind of pure, holy, lovely, just, true and noble thoughts are the seeds of life and peace. Thus we read in Romans 8:6 that to be carnally minded is death; but to be spiritually minded is life and peace.

The Apostle cries out victoriously in what should have

been the last verse of Romans Chapter 7, in 8:2 "For the law of the Spirit of life in Christ Jesus hath made me free from the law of sin and death."

And in culmination of the glorious golden Chapter 8 of Romans declares that not even death can separate him from the love of God in Christ Jesus- Our Lord (8:38).

By Adam came death, by the Second Adam-the Lord from Heaven came the resurrection of the dead (I Cor. 15:21). The last enemy that is death is to be crushed under the feet of Christians by the God of peace, putting out the sting of the Serpent and the victory of the grave (I Cor. 15:54, 55).

Great White Throne Judgment and the Book of Life
Revelation 20:11-15   11 And I saw a great white throne, and him that sat on it, from whose face the earth and the heaven fled away; and there was found no place for them. 12 And I saw the dead, small and great, stand before God; and the books were opened: and another book was opened, which is the book of life: and the dead were judged out of those things which were written in the books, according to their works. 13 And the sea gave up the dead which were in it; and death and Hades delivered up the dead which were in them: and they were judged every man according to their works. 14 And death and hell were cast into the lake of fire. This is the second death. 15 And whosoever

was not found written in the book of life was cast into the lake of fire.

All those who were not among the righteous souls of the Old and New Testament, the unsaved souls of all ages will be resurrected (i.e., clothed with an everlasting body) to stand before the Great White Throne of Almighty God to receive their Judgment. They are judged according to their works. The power of death and the souls contained in the place of the unrighteous dead in Hades will be cast into the Lake of Fire.

Church registration and membership in a denomination do not guarantee salvation. The registration of the soul in the Book of Life in Heaven is the only way to escape the damnation of the everlasting second death. Those who have rejected Jesus in speech and life will be missing in the Book of Life and they will be hurled into the Lake of Fire. This is the Second Death that the Law of God describes as being inevitable to the soul that sins and rejects the atonement in the sinless blood of Jesus.

The second death, in the lake of fire, is as everlasting as the eternal life in heaven. The dimension of time may well be non-existent outside the earthly/cosmic realm. Jesus said that the lake of fire was prepared originally for the devil and his angels (Matthew 25.41).

Gehenna- Valley of Hinnom

To the south of ancient Jerusalem is a precipitous ravine, which stretches down and joins the Valley of Kidron. It was called by the Hebrews, Gei Ben-Hinnom — Ravine (or Valley) of the Son of Hinnom. It was in this valley, at a place called Tophet (probably "place of abomination") that Manasseh and the wicked inhabitants of Jerusalem went to worship idols and to sacrifice their sons and daughters in sacrifice to the god Molech (2 Kgs. 23:10; 2 Ch. 28:3; 33:56; Jer. 7:31; 19:2ff; 32:35; and the apocryphal passage, 1 Enoch 26:1-5).

In fact, the Valley of Hinnom was set aside in Molech's honor. In punishment for the wickedness of the professed people of God, the valley would become the Valley of Slaughter, leaving Judah and Jerusalem desolate. This was literally fulfilled at the destruction of Jerusalem and, according to Jesus' warnings, is a symbol of later punishment. Lake of Fire is the eternal reality, while the symbols of fire and worm used to communicate it are from the Gehenna (or Ge Hinnom) valley where refuse was burnt. The accursed valley was the site of children burnt alive as sacrifices to pagan gods.

In the verses below, speaking about the lake of fire and the everlasting nature of the second death, the Lord Jesus said that the strength of the limbs must be paralysed with regard to sin, instead of going with a whole (everlasting) body that will suffer endless torment in hell.

Matthew 5:29 {BUT IF} {THINE EYE,} {THE} {RIGHT,} {CAUSE TO OFFEND} {THEE,} {PLUCK OUT} {IT} {AND} {CAST [IT]} {FROM} {THEE:} {FOR IT IS PROFITABLE} {FOR THEE} {THAT} {SHOULD PERISH} {ONE} {OF THY MEMBERS,} {AND} {NOT} {WHOLE} {THY BODY} {BE CAST} {INTO} {GEHENNA.}

Matthew 18:9{AND} {IF} {THINE EYE} {CAUSE TO OFFEND} {THEE,} {PLUCK OUT} {IT} {AND} {CAST [IT]} {FROM} {THEE;} {GOOD} {FOR THEE} {IT IS} {ONE EYED} {INTO} {LIFE} {TO ENTER, [RATHER]} {THAN} {TWO} {EYES} {HAVING} {TO BE CAST} {INTO} {THE} {GEHENNA} {OF THE} {FIRE.}

Matthew 5:30 {AND} {IF} {THY RIGHT} {HAND} {CAUSE TO OFFEND} {THEE,} {CUT OFF} {IT} {AND} {CAST [IT]} {FROM} {THEE:} {FOR IT IS PROFITABLE} {FOR THEE} {THAT} {SHOULD PERISH} {ONE} {OF THY MEMBERS,} {AND} {NOT} {WHOLE} {THY BODY} {BE CAST} {INTO} {GEHENNA.}

Mark 9:43{AND} {IF} {SHOULD CAUSE TO OFFEND} {THEE}{THY HAND,} {CUT OFF} {IT:} {GOOD} {FOR THEE} {IT IS} {MAIMED} {INTO}

{LIFE} {TO ENTER, [RATHER]} {THAN} {THE} {TWO} {HANDS}   {HAVING} {TO GO AWAY} {INTO} {THE} {GEHENNA,} {INTO} {THE} {FIRE} {THE} {UNQUENCHABLE}

Mark 9:45 {AND} {IF} {THY FOOT} {SHOULD CAUSE TO OFFEND} {THEE,} {CUT OFF} {IT:} {GOOD} {IT IS} {FOR THEE} <1525> (5629) {TO ENTER} {INTO} {LIFE} {LAME, [RATHER]} {THAN} {THE} {TWO} {FEET} {HAVING} {TO BE CAST} {INTO} {THE} {GEHENNA} {INTO} {THE} {FIRE} {THE} {UNQUENCHABLE}

Mark 9:47 {AND} {IF} {THINE EYE} {SHOULD CAUSE TO OFFEND} {THEE,} {CAST OUT} {IT:} {GOOD} {FOR THEE} {IT IS} {WITH ONE EYE} {TO ENTER} {INTO} {THE} {KINGDOM} {OF GOD, [RATHER]} {THAN} {TWO} {EYES} {HAVING} {TO BE CAST} {INTO} {THE} {GEHENNA} {OF FIRE,}

Compared to that state, Jesus said that making it to heaven, should it even be at the cost of the loss of the (sinful) functions of the eye or the arm (though there is no disability in heaven), is incalculable eternal gain than making it to hell with a whole body. These words make it clear that there is an everlasting body in both heaven and hell.

Reckless Speech and Hellfire

The fires of Hell are directly igniting every form of ungodly speech in our world. To consider or call a brother or fellow man a fool is to risk the judgment of hellfire in the following two verses. In Proverbs 18:21 we read that death and life are in the power of the tongue.

Matthew 5:22 {BUT I} {SAY} {TO YOU,} {THAT} {EVERY ONE} {WHO} {IS ANGRY} {WITH HIS BROTHER} {LIGHTLY} {LIABLE} {SHALL BE} {TO THE} {JUDGMENT:} {BUT WHOEVER} {SHALL SAY} {TO HIS BROTHER,} {RACA,} {LIABLE} {SHALL BE} {TO THE} {SANHEDRIN:} {BUT WHOEVER} {SHALL SAY,} {FOOL,} {LIABLE} SHALL BE TO THE GEHENNA OF FIRE

James the Apostle writes: James 3:6{AND} {THE} {TONGUE [IS]} {FIRE,} {THE} {WORLD} {OF} {UNRIGHTEOUSNESS.} {THUS} {THE} {TONGUE} {IS SET} {IN} {OUR MEMBERS,} {THE} {DEFILER [OF]} {WHOLE} {THE} {BODY,} {AND} {SETTING ON FIRE} {THE} {COURSE} {OF NATURE,} {AND} {BEING SET ON FIRE} {BY} {GEHENNA.}

Destruction

"Destruction" is a word that is used in certain places in the Bible sometimes as a synonym for death and hell. The hearts of all people and all the creation of God are exposed before God, including hell and destruction as we read in Job 26:6 Hell is naked before him, and destruction hath no covering. And again in Proverbs 15:11 Hell and destruction are before the LORD: how much more then the hearts of the children of men?

In 2 Peter 2:1, we read that false prophets and false teachers, who subtly bring in heresies, will deny the Lord that bought them and bring upon themselves swift destruction. The Apostle Peter confirms the divine inspiration of the epistles of Paul, saying that those who are unlearned in scripture and unstable, distort the word of God unto their own destruction.

The infinite capacity of hell to swallow up souls and the eyes of man that covet the things of this world is documented in Proverbs 27:20 Hell and destruction are never full; so the eyes of man are never satisfied.

Uzziah, one of the kings of Judah, took it upon himself to burn incense in the temple of the Lord. This act of arrogance was his destruction for leprosy broke out on his forehead and he died a leper (See 2 Chronicles 26:1-21)

Protection of the Just from Destruction
Among the promises given to those who are corrected by the Lord, we read in Job 5:21 that such a person will be

hidden from the scourge of the tongue and will not be afraid of destruction (when it comes!).

Destruction and the Wicked

Woe unto the wicked when God will put out their candle and when God will distribute sorrows in His anger. The wicked will see their own destruction and will drink of the wrath of Almighty. The wicked is reserved for the day of destruction. They will be brought forth to the day of wrath. (Job 21:17, 20, 30).

The reader of the Bible passage in Job 31: 1-12 is warned that the lustful gazing upon a maiden is wickedness worthy of destruction and a strange punishment awaits those who do such iniquity. The fire of sinful lust of the heart being enticed by any one else than one's own lawful wife is declared to burn all the way to Abaddon.

Job writes that he is terrorized at the thought of the destruction from God and that he would be petrified to immobility because of the Majesty of God, if he had lifted up his hand against an orphan (Job 31:23).

The Psalmist in his prayer for defense from the God of Israel from those who plan his destruction, says in Psalm 35:8 Let destruction come upon him at unawares; and let his net that he hath hid catch himself: into that very destruction let him fall.

Regarding the treacherous and violent men who hunt innocent souls, the Psalmist says in Psalm 55:23 But thou,

O God, shalt bring them down into the pit of destruction: bloodthirsty and deceitful men shall not live out half their days; but I will trust in thee.

The wicked who speak lightly of oppression and who have more than their heart could wish and set their mouth against the heavens are set in slippery places, says Asaph in Psalm 73:18 Surely thou didst set them in slippery places: thou castedst them down into destruction.

He who dwells in the secret place of the Most High and abides under the shadow of the Almighty will not be afraid of the pestilence that walketh in darkness; nor for the destruction that wasteth at noonday as written in Psalm 91:6.

The life of the one who is blessed by the God of Israel as recorded in Psalm 103:4 will be redeemed from destruction and crowned with lovingkindness and tender mercies.

The wisdom of God says that when we do not hearken to the fear of God, then God will not hear us when we call and when our fear comes as desolation, and destruction as a whirlwind (Proverbs 1:27-33). Those who listen to God will dwell safely and securely and will be without fear of evil.

God warns that destruction shall be to the workers of iniquity in Proverbs 10:29 and in Proverbs 10:14 that the mouth of the foolish is near destruction.

A fool's mouth is his own destruction and he that openeth wide his lips will have destruction, as also the one with a spirit of pride will go to destruction and an haughty spirit before a fall. (Proverbs 13:3; 16:18; 18: 7, 12). Before honour is humility.

He that exalts his own position in life is seeking destruction. (Prov. 17:19). Sinners and they that forsake the Lord, as also the workers of iniquity will be destroyed or consumed (Prov. 21:15; Isaiah 1:28). The hearts of evil men study destruction (Pr 24:2).

The enemies of the Cross of Christ are said to have destruction as their end in Philippians 3:19, their God is their belly, their glory is in their shame and they mind earthly things.

The Day of the Lord, as compared to the Day of Christ in Isaiah 13:6 is to come as a destruction from the Almighty. Also Paul in 2 Thessalonians 1:9 says that the Final Advent of the Lord will result in the punishment of everlasting destruction from the presence of the Lord, and from the glory of his power, for those who do not know God and those who do not obey the gospel of Our Lord Jesus Christ.

Sexual Immorality and Second Death
In the first chapter of Paul's epistle to the Romans, we read that the final stage of darkness that seeps into the soul due to

idolatry and ingratitude to God for his gifts of providence and mercy is homosexuality and sexual immorality. Those who do such things not only do this, but also take pleasure in them that do them. (Romans 1:32 Who knowing the judgment of God, that they which commit such things are worthy of death, not only do the same, but have pleasure in them that do them.)

The Adulterer

Job- the Just says in Job 24:15- 25 says that the eye of the adulterer waits for the twilight, saying: No eye will see me, and he disguises his face. Finally, he says that Sheol will consume the adulterers and the worm will feed sweetly on him. Wickedness shall be broken like a tree.

The Immoral Woman- A Minister of Death

The following Scriptures warn all godly men to avoid the immoral woman who is literally a minister of death and hell.

> *Her house is the way to hell,*
> *going down to the chambers of*
> *death. Proverbs 7:27*

And I find more bitter than death the woman,
whose heart is snares and nets, and her hands
as bands: whoso pleases God shall escape
from her; but the sinner shall be taken by her.
Ecclesiastes 7:26

Hypocrisy and Hellfire

Some of the worst judgments will be on hypocrites as Jesus reserved his holy indignation for the Pharisees as missionaries who crossed continents to make converts, only to make them, finally, doubly worthy of hellfire than themselves.

Matthew 23:15   {WOE} {TO YOU,} {SCRIBES} {AND} {PHARISEES,} {HYPOCRITES,} {FOR} {YE GO ABOUT} {THE} {SEA} {AND} {THE} {DRY [LAND]} {TO MAKE} {ONE} {PROSELYTE,} {AND} {WHEN} {HE HAS BECOME [SO],} {YE MAKE} {HIM} {A SON} {OF GEHENNA} {TWOFOLD MORE THAN} {YOURSELVES.}

Matthew 23:33   {SERPENTS,}   {OFFSPRING} {OF VIPERS,} {HOW} {SHALL YE ESCAPE} {FROM} {THE} {JUDGMENT} {OF GEHENNA?}

Gehenna and Judgment of Satan

Revelation 20:10 And the devil that deceived them was cast into the lake of fire and brimstone, where the beast and the false prophet are, and shall be tormented day and night for ever and ever.

Satan (the Adversary of God) or the Devil (Diabolos) will be cast into the Lake of Fire, where the Beast (Antichrist) and the False Prophet have already been thrown.

Isaiah 14:9 Hell from beneath is moved for thee to meet thee at thy coming: it stirreth up the dead for thee, even all the chief ones of the earth; it hath raised up from their thrones all the kings of the nations. {chief...: Heb. leaders, or, great goats}

Isaiah 14:11 Thy pomp is brought down to the grave, and the noise of thy viols: the worm is spread under thee, and the worms cover thee.

Isaiah 14:19 But thou art cast out of thy grave like an abominable branch, and as the raiment of those that are slain, thrust through with a sword, that go down to the stones of the pit; as a carcase trodden under feet.

Note that it is written in Revelation 14:11 And the smoke of their torment ascends up for ever and ever: and they have no rest day nor night, who worship the beast and his image, and whosoever receives the mark of his name (i.e., the name of the number of the Beast- 666).

This torment is referred to in Revelation 14.10 as drinking of the "...wine of the wrath of God, which is poured out without mixture into the cup of his indignation; and he shall be tormented with fire and brimstone in the presence of the holy angels, and in the presence of the Lamb:"

Those who partake in the First Resurrection, in the various orders after the Resurrection and Ascension of Jesus, are considered blessed and upon them the second death shall have no power, but they shall be priests of God and of Christ, and shall reign with him a thousand years (Revelation. 20:6). They cease from their labours and their works follow after them (Revelation 14.13). From the latter verse, we understand that the righteous deeds of the saints follow their souls into eternity.

The list of the kind of wicked souls that will populate the lake which burns with fire and brimstone and makes up the second death is given in Revelation 21:8: ..the fearful, and unbelieving, and the abominable, and murderers, and whoremongers, and sorcerers, and idolaters, and all liars…

Outside the blessed and holy city- New Jerusalem are dogs, and sorcerers, and whoremongers, and murderers, and idolaters, and whosoever loveth and maketh a lie (Revelation 22.15).

Outer Darkness
In Matthew 13.42, we read of an outer darkness where there will be bitter regret accompanied with "weeping, wailing and grinding of teeth". It is believed by many

Christians that the eternal destiny of this place and the souls assigned there will be united with Gehenna.

The Spirit-baptized believers, making up the New Testament Church, are by the grace of God urged to prepare to meet their Glorious God. After the Second Coming of Christ, they will have to face Christ at His Judgment Seat, to obtain their rewards, according as our works have been. God does not want us to be rejected so as to even face the dire consequence of being hurt by the second death.

The parting words of the Risen Christ, in the clear words of prophecy of the last book of the Bible, are urging us to be more righteous and holy than we are now, and promising us that if we do His commandments we will have access to the tree of life, and may enter in through the gates into the heavenly city.

Thus says: the Alpha and Omega, the beginning and the end, the first and the last.

The Christian has a Glorious Assurance in the words "O death where is thy sting, O grave where is thy victory.", and in the challenge of Jesus: O death, I will be thy plagues.

May those, who acknowledge these things, say with the Holy Spirit and the Bride of Christ, unto the King of Kings and Lord of Lords: Even so, come, Lord Jesus.

May we receive the grace of our Lord Jesus Christ

that will cause us to watch and pray so that we may be accounted worthy to escape all these things and to stand before the Son of Man.

The Blessed Hope of every Christian is given in Revelation 21:4 And God shall wipe away all tears from their eyes; and there shall be no more death, neither sorrow, nor crying, neither shall there be any more pain: for the former things are passed away.

To the Christian Reader who may seek to walk closer to the Lord of Life, these are the words over every Christian grave:

There is no death.
No. Not for the Christian!
Only an honourable discharge from life's battles,

A promotion to duties in Heaven,
That glorious moment to step forward
And hear the Great Commander-in-Chief say,
"Well done, good and faithful soldier!
Come, enter into your Eternal reward"!

There is no death. Not for the Christian.
Only the soul's blessed release from prison.
Only a passage out of that prison into a palace.

Only a golden key that unlocks
the treasures of Eternity.

No, my friend, you are not dead.
You have gone higher, that is all.
Out of this old mud shack,
into a house that is immortal,
A body that no enemy can attack!
"Dust thou art, to dust thou shalt return"
Was not spoken of the spirit.
You don't really die, you just keep on living,
And go straight into the presence of the Lord!

I weep, dear friend, because I miss you.
If I were unselfish I would be rejoicing with you,
Thanking God that you are with Him!
Thanking God that your troubles are over!
No more crying, no more pain, no more sorrow,
Nothing but eternal happiness in Heaven forever!
Yes, we are so selfish about death,
We count our grief far more than your joy!
So for now, farewell, my friend!
We shall meet again!

To every reader of this book, be informed that this book is a warning to escape from the Way of Death and Hell and endeavour to go the narrow way of Life with the Lord Jesus.

And unto this people thou shall say,
Thus says the LORD; Behold, I set before you
the way of life, and the way of death.
Jeremiah 21:8

Let all that has breath praise the Lord.
Amen.

Appendix – I

How about Abortion and Capital Punishment?

The Encyclopedia of World History (2001) reports that early Christians condemned infant exposure, abortion, and capital punishment—all widely practiced in the ancient world. John Piper concludes that if the actual events of abortion and capital punishment (such as execution in the electric chair) were featured in the national media at prime time, it would wipe out the evil practices.

God in Jesus Christ of Nazareth, has forgiven all my sins even the murder of an unborn baby. This book is the sincere fruit of my repentant heart to every person who may not be aware of the fact that the soul is formed at conception in the womb. The uncertainty over the law of God led to my acceptance of the ungodly medical advice to terminate the life of a baby with Down's syndrome.

The provoked abortion that my wife and I agreed to proceed with, at the hospital in Copenhagen, was nothing less than murder. It was actively encouraged by the medical authorities in a public policy that aimed to avoid spending money on the care of a child with Down's syndrome. We have a second child in heaven as an eternal testimony of our heinous act and the mercy of God that has forgiven us the terrible sin.

The cry of my heart today is that all people on earth may know that abortion is awfully contrary to the Law of God. I have, since then, read the reports of several who have witnessed the Infants Paradise in heaven where children are gathering in from around the world in everlasting testimony to the cruelty of earthly fathers and mothers.

It is because I have come to tangibly feel the sorrow and pain of the Wounded Heart of my Father in Heaven, His unfathomable love for every soul on the face of the earth that makes me prepare this warning and legacy for anyone who will ever read this book.

We can fool others and even ourselves, but we cannot fool God. We can play church and end up in everlasting hellfire. We can pretend to be Christians and put up a beautiful exterior, when the pit of Hell inspires our innermost thoughts and intentions of what we say and do.

It is paradoxical that the governments that protect the rights of the child are actively promoting the murder of the unborn baby. The Church ought to be deeply ashamed for its failure in denouncing the evil genocide of abortion.

Abortion is a monstrous evil that is outrageous to God. From the beginning to the end of sacred Scripture, there is a premium on the sanctity of human life. Human life is cheapened in the wanton destruction of unborn children. From a biblical standpoint, the issue focuses on the origin of life. It would be merely sophistry to call it murder, if in fact it was not the killing of human life.

The biblical evidence is manifold that life begins at conception. We see that repeatedly in the literature of the prophets in the Old Testament, in the psalms of David, and in the New Testament where at the meeting of Elizabeth and Mary, after she has conceived Jesus, John the Baptist, as yet unborn, bears witness to the presence of the Messiah, who also is not yet born. Neither one of these are born infants, and yet there is communication taking place.

The prophet Jeremiah and the apostle Paul both speak of being consecrated and sanctified, while they were still in their mothers' wombs. These and a host of other passages indicate clearly that life begins before birth and at conception.

Appendix - II

How can we face death cheerfully?

There is a saying, "Everybody wants to go to heaven, but nobody wants to die!" For some, the very word death is frightening. If the Lord tarries, one day we all have to die, it can take place even today. It is therefore very essential that we be always prepared for it. It is very true in the spiritual sense that "those who are ready to die are the ones who are ready to live."

If we have to face death cheerfully, in the first place, we must make sure that there is absolutely no unconfessed, or hidden secret sins in our life. The Blood of Jesus has no power to cleanse unconfessed or unrepented sins in our life. "The Blood of Jesus Christ His Son cleanseth us from all sin....If we confess our sins, He is faithful and just to forgive us our sins and to cleanse us from all unrighteousness" (1 John 1:7,9).

If we keep unwashed hidden sins in our life, what will happen at the time of our death? EVERY HIDDEN SIN, at the time of death, will turn out to be a sting that will STING OUR SOUL, SPIRIT AND BODY

SIMULTANEOUSLY. That is why we read, "O death, where is thy sting? ... . The sting of death is sin..." (1 Cor 15:55-56).

Those who keep such unwashed hidden sins, when they die, their death is called, "bitterness of death" (1 Sam 15:32), "sorrows of death" (Psa 18:4), "snares of death" (Psa 18:5), "destruction of death" (Job 28:22), "terrors of death" (Psa 55:4), "grievous death" (Jer 16:4), etc.

Very often, many people of God may hide bitterness, unforgiving spirit, hatred, envy, anger, arrogant pride, greed, etc., in their heart and may pretend to be loving, forgiving, gentle, gracious, etc. BUT WHILE DYING NO ONE CAN PRETEND as every sin like a sting will be tormenting that person. "Your sin will find you out."

However, those saints who are washed fully in the blood of the Lamb and walk with God without hiding any sin, their death is called sweet sleep - "thy sleep shall be sweet" (Pro 3:24). Jesus "by the grace of God [tasted] death" (Heb 2:9). Here the word 'tasted' signifies like tasting honey. Yes, for saints who live a transparent life, death will be sweet like honey, as the bitterness of death was taken away by the death of our Lord Jesus Christ.

For true saints, death is the most wonderful moment, meeting our most blessed Saviour. It was no surprise that St. Paul shouted, "For to me ... to die is gain" (Phil 1:21). What is this gain? Saints fully inherit and gain Jesus eternally only at the time of death. Can we get any better gain than gaining Jesus? See the last words of the great saint D.L. Moody: "This is my coronation day. If this is called death, how sweet it is." One day F. F. Bosworth (a great man of God) announced, "This is the greatest day of my life. God has shown me that I am going home." That same day he peacefully went to be with the Lord. He was well over eighty.

Dear reader, it is not worth keeping any sin hidden in your life. Why should you keep stings hidden in your heart, knowing that one day they are going to torment you? Why don't you make a decision to bring to light every hidden sin, repent of them and walk with God with all humility and purity. If so, not only will you be able face death cheerfully at any time, but also, the testimony of your sweet sleep will make others to follow your sweet Saviour all the way to glory.

Source: Hidden Manna June 2004,
The Pentecostal Mission (TPM), Chennai, India

Appendix – III

Can a Christian be Cremated?

Once a saint dies, whether the body is buried or disposed of by any other means, it does not affect the eternal blessing of his soul. There were saints who were burned alive and some others eaten by lions. They are all safe in heaven.

According to the Encyclopedia Britannica, cremation is of pagan origin. The Word of God discloses that 'burning' is a sign of God's Judgment and curse. The dead body of King Saul (who displeased God) was not buried but burnt (1 Sam 31:12). The burning of human bones was a most serious crime of Moab. (Amos 2:1,2). Harlots were to be burnt (Gen 38:24; Lev 21:9). Achan, who had stolen the accursed things had to be burnt with fire (Josh 7:15, 25).

When the wicked queen Jezebel was killed, there was no one to bury her (2 Kings 9:10). In the Old Testament, the phrase "Thou shalt be gathered to thy grave in peace" was a sign of God's great blessing (2 Chron 34:27,28; 35:24).

In the New Testament, John the Baptist, Stephen, etc. were buried (Matt 14:12; Acts 8:2). Above all, Jesus was buried according to the Scriptures (1 Cor 15:4). In 1 Corinthians 15:35-44, St. Paul narrates beautifully as to why a Christian should be buried and what a blessed hope of resurrection it signifies.

In conclusion, burning of bodies is associated in the Scriptures with the judgment and curse of God. We all should follow Christ's own example of burial. According to God's Word, burial shows that a body is a seed to be sown in corruption but raised in incorruption and this beautiful figure is utterly lost in cremation.

Source: Hidden Manna, February 2004.

The Pentecostal Mission, Chennai, India.

Appendix - IV

How is life in hell (Lake of Fire)?

There are quite a number of people who do not believe in heaven or hell. But that doesn't change the fact that they exist. I may say, "I don't believe in the Himalayan mountains. I haven't seen them, and so I don't believe they exist," but the Himalayan mountains still stand high. Whether you believe in heaven and hell, or not, heaven and hell exist.

If your life is a drama, the last scene of the drama is mentioned in Revelation chapter 20. "I saw a great white throne" (v. 11). God's throne is called a 'white' throne. White stands for purity. On the final day of judgment the only difference that will be seen is the difference between saints and sinners. Whether men or women, rich or poor, literate or illiterate, great or small, there will be no difference on the day of judgment—the only difference will be between the holy and the unholy.

"And I saw Him that sat on it." He is our Lord Jesus Christ. Today Jesus is calling everyone saying, "Come unto Me and I will give you rest." Now if you reject this invitation to come to Christ, one day the same Jesus will be Judge and He will say, "Depart from Me, you workers of iniquity...." "And I saw the dead small and great stand before God" (v. 12). Whether you are a great politician, a rich man, a businessman, a small man or a great man, you will have to stand before the judgment seat of Christ.

"And the books were opened." Today your life may be like a closed book. Nobody has seen all the secret sins you have committed. But they are all recorded in a book and that book is going to be opened one day. If your life is not an open book now, one day it will be opened, and it will be only to judge and not to bless. You may be saved, you may have received the Holy Spirit, but still your life may be a closed book. Another book, the Book of Life, is also opened. Why is that book called the Book of Life? In a spiritual sense, all sinners are dead.

This book is called the Book of Life because the names of those who got new life, the life of God, through salvation, are written in it. You may have been saved fifty years ago, you may have taken water baptism and received the Holy Spirit, and you may be living a very good life in the outward way. But the day you commit sin and hide it without repenting and confessing it, your name will be blotted out of the Book of Life.

One Christian lady, Mary Baxter, had visions of heaven and hell. She was shocked to see in hell many Sunday School teachers, youth leaders, pastors, great preachers, prophets, singers, etc. They had been hypocrites. Dear reader, don't wait for the Day of Judgment to open your book.

"The dead were judged out of those things which are written in the books, according to their works." Everybody is not going to have equal suffering in hell. The punishments or the judgment will differ according to each one's works. Proverbs 9:18 says that immoral people, those who commit fornication, adultery, etc. will be in the depths of hell or in the hottest place in hell. That is why David who committed sin with Bathsheba says, after God forgave him, "He delivered me out of the lowest hell."

Dear friend, don't go to the depths of hell, to the hottest place in hell. One day your sin will find you out. You cannot hide your sin for very long. The judgment of God is going to come on even immoral thoughts and looks. So, O child of God, show a zeal and love for purity of life. "And the sea gave up the dead which were in it." Those who died in the sea will all be delivered up for the judgment. "And death and hell delivered up the dead which were in them."

Sinners and backsliders go to these places of torment as soon as they die and there they await judgment. A person who has committed a crime is first remanded to custody before he is judged and condemned, isn't he? It's like that. "And death and hell were cast into the lake of fire. This is the second death." Why is it called the second death? Death means separation. When the prodigal son returned home the father said, "This my son was dead." That is, he had been separated from the father. Physical death is the soul and spirit getting separated from this physical body. The second death is the dead people getting eternally separated from God.

The Word of God tells us what type of life people will have in hell. According to the Word of God they will be suffering in hell in three ways. First, thinking about their past—what they lost, for example, will bring suffering. Secondly, there is their existing suffering—what they are undergoing at the moment. Thirdly, thoughts about their future suffering—what they are going to go through, will give them suffering.

In hell, people will regret all they have lost. They have lost the blessed presence of God forever. This is what really makes hell. They have lost the company of the holy angels forever. And they have lost the fellowship of the true saints. All they have with them now is the demons that torment them. They have lost heaven, the most blessed place in Eternity. Their constant thought is, "O, never will heaven's gate be opened for me—not even for one second!" In hell everyone is disappointed—"I had a lot of opportunities to come to God, to receive forgiveness, to accept Christ, but I rejected them all." The mind will be tormented with such thoughts.

There is a real story in the Bible of a man who went to hell—the story of the rich man and Lazarus in Luke chapter 16. The 25th verse is really a cutting verse. Abraham says to the rich man, "Son, remember that you in your lifetime received the good things." In hell the rich man had quite a lot of time to "remember." On earth he must have been very busy—he had no time for God. In hell people will get enough time to remember how many times they rejected the counsel of the saints, how many times God had urged them to take the right water baptism, how many times God had warned them to change their character, how many times God and the saints had pleaded with them to give up their smoking, drinking, and immorality, how much money they wasted on the vanities and comforts of the world, etc. Remembering all these things in hell will be too late; it will only bring torment. That will not help you at all, dear friend.

Also, the suffering one continuously undergoes in hell each moment is indescribable. There is so much fire that even if all the water in the whole world is poured into hell, the fire cannot be quenched. There is no rest or peace there. Pain in hell will be such that no words can express it. The people in hell are tormented not only by the fire, but in a million other ways too. When a person has a splitting headache or chest pain, his hands and feet may be alright and so the pain is, in a way, bearable. But in hell, every part of the body, from head to foot, will be tormented to the utmost in every possible way, every single moment.

People who are suffering on earth manage to get a little relief through at least a little sleep, but those in hell will not have even a wink of sleep or rest for all Eternity. One simply cannot do anything—cannot sit, cannot walk, cannot lie down. In addition, there is the torture from 'worms that die not.' Isaiah 14:11 says that there are worms under them and worms covering them all over! And all those worms will be stinging them. They cannot rid themselves of the worms as their hands and feet are bound with fetters.

They will also have to constantly keep seeing the horrifying sights of the grotesque ugly demons and the sight of others being tortured most inhumanly. Dark smoke will suffocate them—taking each breath would be as agonizing as if one were breathing his last. The loud shrieks of the demons and the screaming and groaning and wailing of the damned souls in hell will keep ringing in their ears all the time. And imagine the awful smells one has to endure there—the strong smell of the burning sulphur, the foul stench of burning and decomposing flesh, etc. Extreme and unquenchable thirst is another unbearable suffering in hell—there being not even a drop of water there.

Another thing is that, although hell will be crowded, everyone will be lonely there. Everyone there will be hating one another. Even a family of a husband, wife and children who loved one another very much while on earth would start hating one another with perfect hatred as soon as they land in hell. In hell nobody will be caring, loving, helping, understanding or compassionate. Backsliders will have worse torment than sinners. Of backsliders we read that they will be bound hand and foot and thrown into outer darkness. Friend, if you have gone back after receiving Jesus, heed Jesus calling you back to Himself today. Revelation chapter 16 says that the darkness in hell will be a tormenting fire-like darkness. Everyone will be gnashing their teeth, cursing themselves and God for their terrible plight.

Another terrible torment one has in hell is in looking to the future. Those in hell know that their misery will never have an end. When they think of their future they have no better place, no better condition, nothing at all to hope for. Even the most miserable person on earth has some hope to live for. But those who are in hell are absolutely hopeless. They have lost all hope of ever receiving forgiveness for their sins, all hope of getting any mercy or help from any source, of finding comfort or blessing even in the remote future.

On earth, the gates of even the worst prison are open for at least a short time every day. But the people in hell know that their doors, their gates will never be opened. Never will the burning chains be removed. There will be no breaking away from the suffering even after ten million ages. The sufferings are only going to increase. This very thought will be all the more tormenting.

In the 16th chapter of Luke we find some frightening facts about hell fire. As soon as the rich man entered hell, the first part of his body that appeared to have been tormented, was his tongue. In the 24th verse we read he cried and said, "Father Abraham, have mercy on me and send Lazarus that he may dip the tip of his finger in water and cool my tongue, for I am tormented in the flame." Although the whole body was tormented, particular mention is made about the torment of the tongue. The Word of God says, "The tongue is a fire, a world of iniquity." Why is it written 'a world of iniquity'?

Your tongue creates your heaven or hell. If your marriage is hell, it is because your tongue is hell. If your family is hell, it means your tongue is hell. How many times has your tongue set others on fire! I Peter 3:10 very clearly says that if your tongue is evil, your future is going to be evil. If you often speak evil of others, you can expect a grim future. Abraham's reply to Lazarus's request was, "Impossible." This shows that praying to great saints or to dead people is in vain. One of the greatest saints of the Old Testament was Abraham. But the prayer made to him was not answered.

Heaven, in contrast to hell, is a place of lasting joy, peace, grace and love. In hell, one has to endure all the wrath of all the demons; in heaven, one enjoys all the goodness of the Lord. Saints will be comforted in heaven in three ways. Thinking about their past, they will be grateful to the Lord for wonderfully saving them, keeping them from backsliding till death, keeping them in the numerous trials they faced, helping them to take water baptism, receive the Holy Spirit and walk with Him, etc.

Looking at their present comfort, they will greatly rejoice beholding the glorious face of the One they love, the beauties of heaven, the joyful faces of all the saints in heaven and the beautiful holy angels, listening to the sweet words of Jesus, and the melodious music and singing and the praises of the saints and the angels, and enjoying the pleasant aroma. There will be no pain, no sorrow, no death, no devil, and nothing to fear.

They will also rejoice looking into the future, in heaven, knowing that all their present joys and blessings are going to keep increasing more and more as days go by, knowing that they are going to keep growing in the grace of God, in the wisdom of God, in the knowledge of God, etc. Beloved one, eye has not seen, nor ear heard, nor has entered into the heart of man, all that the Lord has prepared for us in heaven.

"Why is hell eternal? Why would a loving God want to torment people with such unbearable tortures for all Eternity?", you may ask. God is not only a loving God, but also a righteous Judge. If the Lord gives eternal comfort and blessings to those who accept Him and obey Him, His righteousness demands that eternal torments be given to those who reject Him and disobey Him.

Precious friend, you have a very precious soul. Once you close your eyes your destiny is determined and sealed. It will be too late to repent or turn to God after that. If your life is a closed book, open it today. Let heaven come into your heart right now. Get the assurance that if you close your eyes now, you will be with Jesus in heaven.

Jesus is tenderly inviting you. He is waiting to wash your sins and forgive all your iniquities. Please come to Him, open your heart and confess all your sins. He will be merciful to you and bless you. If you hear His voice today, don't harden your heart.

Source: Hidden Manna, August 2005. The Pentecostal Mission TPM, Chennai, India.

Appendix - V

What will happen if a Christian commits suicide?
Whether a Christian or non-Christian takes his own life
or another's it is murder. "No murderer has eternal life
abiding in him" (1 Jn 3:15).

It is crystal clear from the Scriptures that Satan
entered into Judas Iscariot before he betrayed Jesus and
then committed suicide (Jn 13:27). Anyone who takes his
own life is no better than Judas Iscariot.

In the Bible, the men who committed suicide were
terrible backsliders such as king Saul, Ahithophel, Judas
Iscariot, etc.

If a sinner commits suicide, he may go to hell. But
when a born-again Christian commits suicide he will
go to a worse place called outer darkness, the place for
backsliders. In outer darkness there willl be more torment
than in hell and there will be weeping and gnashing of
teeth (Matt 8:12).

Suicide is not the shortcut to heaven as some foolishly
think. It is not a way of escape to the place "where all
the problems are gone." On the other hand it is virtually

falling "from the frying pan to the fire"- even to the Lake of fire. Let no sincere born again Christian ever imagine that he will be safe in heaven after ending his life in this way.

It is true that God is gracious, compassionate and forgiving. But once a person commits suicide he doesn't get a chance to repent and turn to God. There are some exceptional cases where the person does not die immediately and lingers, so that he can repent and ask for forgiveness from the Lord. But such cases are very rare. While alive, if anybody genuinely repents for any sin he will receive forgiveness.

Perhaps someone who is reading these lines may be facing a temptation to commit suicide. Dear friend, not only your soul will be in eternal torment but the Lord's name will also be greatly blasphemed through this shameful and sinful act. Today the gracious Lord is calling you, "Come unto Me, all ye that labour and are heavy laden and I will give you rest." You can cast all your care upon Him "for He careth for you." "God is our refuge and strength and a very present help in trouble." He promises that in your temptations He will "make a way to escape" that you may be able to bear it (1Cor 10:13).

Open your heart to Jesus, He understands your pain. He is the Good Samaritan. He will pour in oil and wine and bind up all your wounds. Please pray that the good

Lord will remove the very thought of suicide from you, and that He may graciously forgive you and give you new life.

"Therefore if any man be in Christ He is a new creature: Old things are passed away; behold, all things are become new" (2Cor.5:17).

Source: Hidden Manna. The Pentecostal Mission TPM, Chennai, India.

Appendix – VI

What happens to children who die before they can accept the gospel?

Christians believe that those children who die in infancy are numbered among the redeemed. That is to say, we hope and have a certain level of confidence that God will be particularly gracious toward those who have never had the opportunity to be exposed to the gospel, such as infants or children who are too disabled to hear and understand.

The New Testament does not teach us this explicitly. It does tell us a lot about the character of God—about his mercy and his grace—and gives us every reason to have that confidence in his dealings with children. Some Christians however have the pagan practice of baptizing infants, possibly due to fears that original sin will condemn infants to eternal damnation.

Infants who die are given a special dispensation of the grace of God, as we see David's situation in the Old Testament when his infant child dies. Yet David is given the confidence that he will see that child again in heaven.

This account is of much consolation to parents who have lost babies in spontaneous abortions or children in their infancy.

Appendix – VII

Are those who have never heard of Christ going to hell?

"How could God ever possibly send some person to hell who never even had the opportunity to hear of the Saviour? It just doesn't seem right.

At the outset of his epistle to the Romans, the apostle Paul points out that the righteous wrath of God is manifested against all ungodliness and unrighteousness. God is not angry with innocent people, but God hates evil. God expects all people everywhere to acknowledge, worship and seek to know the God whose attributes are amply manifested in nature.

God is clearly revealed in the visible Universe as the Invisible, Omnipotent and Omniscient Creator worthy of worship. Every human being knows that there is a God and that he is accountable to God. Yet every human being disobeys God. It is evil to reject the self-disclosure of God.

Idolatry is described as the result of the darkness that comes from ungratefulness to the providence of God. Idolaters are among those who will have their part in Hell.

The Good News or Gospel of Jesus Christ is the marvellous story of redemption that God has provided for humanity. Christ was sent into a world that is on its way to hell to reveal the glory of God's grace, the extent to which God has gone to redeem us. The Sovereign Lord can unilaterally grant His mercy to an ignorant soul, but there are no innocent souls and hence the serious and urgent commission of Christ to go into all the world and tell them of Jesus.

Appendix – VIII

LIFE, DEATH AND RESURRECTION

'A TIMELINE'

- **'Former' Eternity** John 1:1
  God of Love (Goodness & Light = No beginning or end.)
- **Creation of Angels (With beginning, but no end)**
  Col. 1:16
- **Fall of Satan (Darkness/Evil begins)**
  Cast down from Heaven. Isaiah 14:15
  To be finally consigned to the Lake of Fire.
- **Sin and Death through First Adam.** Romans 5:12
  Fall of Adam = Spiritual death / Loss of Eternal life
- **Reconciliation & Eternal Life through Last Adam**
  Jesus Christ of Nazareth- Life and Ministry II Tim. 1:10
  Appearance of Jesus = Eternal Life and Immortality
  Death of Jesus = Second Death abolished for believers.
  Resurrection and Ascension of Jesus = Justification

- **Dispensation of Grace / New Testament Church**
- **Rapture of Bride of Christ / Resurrection of living and dead saints.** I Thess. 4:16, 17
- **Judgment Seat of Christ = Rewards for N. Testament Believers.**
- **Tribulation Period (7 years).** Rev. 12:6
  Martyrdom of faithful believers. Rev. 12:13-17
  Martyrdom and Resurrection of Enoch and Elijah
  144,000 Jewish believers preserved from bodily death
  to enter the Millennial Reign.
- **Millennial Reign of Christ on earth**   Rev. 20:2-4
  Power of bodily death and sin largely curtailed Satan
  bound in the Bottomless Pit for 1000 years.
  Resurrection of Old Testament saints and general
  martyrs.
- **White Throne Judgment (Sheep and Goats)** Rev.
  20:13
- **New Earth = Souls with names in Book of Life.** Rev.
  21:1
- **Lake of Fire and Brimstone = Second Death**   Rev.
  20:14
  Souls whose names are NOT found in the Book of
  Life.
- **'Latter' Eternity: Kingdom of The Father** I Cor. 15:24
  Fullness of Life & Glory = No sin, sickness, death, pain
  or sorrow.

Maafa: KiSwahili for Horror or Holocaust. Europe is yet to compensate and reconcile with Africa for the 24-30 million slaves that were plundered in the depopulation of Africa in the Transatlantic Slave Trade during the so-called period of Enlightenment in Europe! Denmark accounted for 200,000 African souls in this horrendous trade.

The children of slaves and their produce are now being kept out of Europe and North America, while the cotton, cane sugar, coffee, cocoa, bananas etc., are imported at grossly unfair prices, besides the evil subsidies given by the OECD to cotton, sugar, rice, etc., The fence around the European Union is so effective that people are falling from airplanes, getting choked in trucks and crossing the Sahara in vain.

Dalit: The racist oppression of the ex-untouchables, over 200 million dalits, besides the over 70 million adivasis (first dwellers) in South Asia, calls for another liberation. The dalits are reckoned less than animals by many caste Hindus. The caste system consists of the brahmin priests, rulers, merchants and workers. The oppression of the untouchables outside the caste spectrum is based on an upward scale of awe and downward scale of contempt with religious sanction.

May Europe be reconciled with Africa
May the Dalits of South Asia find true freedom.
May all men be free in knowing Truth that God is Love.